Phoenix Rising

A Life in the Cla

1995 - 202

By Martyn Agass

Contents

PGCE Hull University 1995 -1996

St Mary's College Mixed Comprehensive

Don't look when crossing the playground. An early lesson.

GCSE economics is so boring.

Bridlington Mixed Comprehensive

I want to be a deck chair attendant when I grow up.

Let's check you have in fact changed the OHP bulb.

Don't worry if you don't get the job.

Split sites.

Flashcards.

Get a grip man.

Paderborn.

Wonderwall minibus.

The early years 1996 - 2008

Northwood Hills Mixed Comprehensive

GCSE business studies and 3 in 1 lesson.

Love You.

I'll just be in the office taking a phone call.

Aussie backpackers.

All the best teachers eventually leave.

Just sit still on your stool.

Leave Jennings alone.

Wheelie chair racing.

Smoker's heaven.

Where is Stevo?

Skin head charity haircut.

You didn't buy a plastic rose?

The kitchen sink.

The Green Man.

I've been food poisoned.

The Aquarium.

It's time to leave pronto.

Orange swirls.

Invigilating A-level exams.

Going Nowhere Very Quickly.

Zoe has been on roll since.

Parent's evening.

Hammersmith.

We are the champions and a brick through the window.

Aqua plaining.

What is that quiver on your back?

Northern Ireland

Larne Grammar School Mixed Grammar

Just got off the boat, he's teaching The Battle of Hastings.

Carrickfergus College Mixed Comprehensive

What's the name of the head of year?

Bloomfield Collegiate All Girls Grammar

The Pink Palace.

Anyone for 5-a-side?

Castlereigh Mixed FE College

Can adults do an A-level in 2 hours a week in one year?

Wallace High School Mixed Grammar

Why am I still teaching french?

Normandy and Paris.

Talk and coloured chalk.

Christmas panto, 7 dwarfs.

No surrender, putting the great back into Great Britain.

Anyone for a game of snooker?

Belfast pub crawls.

Where's the nearest toilet? Quick.

School formal.

Oh my god, what was that drink you just gave me?

I have a bone to pick with you.

Zonal marking.

Schools Cup final.

We stuffed you at rugby assembly.

A bit of careers.

Work experience – Fleming Fulton.

Let's play chess.

All Ireland MUN.

R&J.

The Entitlement Framework. This is the end.

The Office & staring into the abyss.

The middle years 2008 – 2012

Carrickfergus Mixed Grammar

What a tail. Call that a grammar.

Malone Integrated College Mixed Comprehensive

Different directions on the bell at the end of school.

It must be good for NI.

Dundonald High School Mixed Comprehensive

Separate staff rooms and why are you here, we're probably closing.

St Columbas College Catholic Mixed Comprehensive

Prayer beads and welcome.

Ballyclare Mixed Grammar

Cosy country grammar with another snooker table.

Hydepark Brethren Mixed Comprehensive

Accountancy calling.

Let's start from scratch.

A different theory of evolution.

Sexist hypocrites.

Up against the wall.

Newtownbreda High School Mixed Comprehensive

She went to Purdysburn.

Maths anybody? How about Office Communication Systems? A bit of ICT.

No. They just stop us.

Girlie fight.

The removal room.

A-level examiner.

On a drip.

Would you like to try the big chair?

Don't peuk up on me!

Royal School Dungannon Mixed Grammar

Time for geography and more ICT.

Radio 2 breakfast show.

Let me google check that football trivia, despite you saying you watched it live.

God loves you, but you'll all burn in hell and damnation.

Facilitate this.

Dorm rota.

Tripping out.

If the cuts continue, then I'll be forced to hang 'closed' on the school gates.

London Calling

Bellerbey's College Mixed International

No uniform after all these years.

Open plan office.

I wanna be like you when I grow up.

Killer commute & Haut-Médoc.

The Cutty Sark and Greenwich.

Who's got talent?

Mismatching summer holidays.

The later years 2012 – 2022

ACS Mixed International

I'm not your HOD, just your mentor.

Do what you want, so long as the parents don't complain.

IB.

Finally, some history.

GPA.

My dad is on the politburo and says the papers are wrong.

Helipads and lockdown drills.

Bomb scare.

Suleman.

The Merchant of Death.

£15000 is not enough.

The Prince of Montenegro.

Ewell Castle All Boys Private

HOD.

Now it's also politics.

3 teachers per course.

It's a nice office but why am I here? Just watch me get out of this one.

You belong with the sixth form.

ACS Mixed International Continued

A 2nd homecoming.

One step at a time - Welkernomics.

Going big with business management.

We are Chelsea FC.

I'll tell Andy Murray; he's, my neighbour.

Coursework panic.

Tutoring.

Office mates, displays and coffee talk.

Ypres and the trenches.

HMS Victory. Chessington, The Wave of Terror, Theatreland.

Pac-Man invigilation.

ACS graduation & how the other half live.

Berlin and Paris.

Cost cutting.

The Old Dorm & whiskey nights.

Woodlands Phoenix.

Morning coffee and walks through the woods.

The Flintstones.

You cannot be serious! The human shield.

The Covid years.

For those who walked.

750 flights later Lord Centurion.

Grosvenor Mixed Grammar

A work in progress.

Whatever happened to the Cayman Islands or somewhere else exotic?

There's no place like home.

Recollections

<u>Extra Time 2022 – 2025</u>

Campbell College All Boys Grammar

Parachuted in. No rest for the wicked.

Hogwarts.

The cream of Ulster.

Larne High School Mixed Comprehensive

Commuting made easy.

What did they do to the state sector? Underfunding, fall in pay.

Humane headmaster. As it should be.

Pupil low self-esteem. Poor behaviour.

Teaching assistants.

Plugging the gap.

A job and no longer a vocation.

We're all out on strike.

Sledgehammer Day.

Where next?

The irony of no longer commuting.

Larne Grammar School Mixed Grammar Revisited

Back to LGS to see my wife.

Why was economics mainly axed in NI?

St Louise's Catholic Mixed Comprehensive

Falls Road.

Helping in business studies.

Maths and KS3.

Where are you from in England?

Starting to feel better.

Hail Mary staff training.

Staff room table and up the revolution.

Completely skint and having to tutor.

It's Christmas!

Belfast High School Mixed Grammar

Pleasant kids.

An old acquaintance.

Next generation. This is approaching the end my friend.

Semi-Retiring

Edmund Rice College Catholic Mixed Comprehensive

Pleasant week with staff and kids.

Victoria College All Girls Grammar

Artificial Intelligence.

My wife's childhood school.

Perfect school for semi-retiring. Full circle and back home.

Phoenix time, rising from the ashes?

What came next, and then ....

Phoenix Rising

A Life in the Classroom

1995 - 2025

By Martyn Agass

I sometimes ask myself, why did you want to become a teacher? Well, I guess there are the holidays and the fact that you might get to help steer young minds in the right direction, but then the pay is not the best especially considering it's meant to be a profession. It's not the worst pay either when you look around at all those struggling in low paid dead-end jobs, so I should be grateful, but still for what we do teachers are under paid. Nearly everyone is in society, the top bosses see to that. The question remains though, why teaching? In many ways the answer is not having contacts and connections to open doors and launch into a family business or some unpaid internship to gain invaluable early career experience. Teaching is a career where you can still make it on your own endeavours. Maybe I just have a calling to be a teacher and have found my vocation in life, or maybe I just didn't want a boring office job. I think I would rather have been a rock star, but then again wouldn't everybody want the dream of being a rockstar? Dreams are not always what they are made out to be.

What I did learn though was that it is often more about the journey than the destination. My teaching career has been one long journey.

PGCE Hull University 1995 - 1996

"What do you mean this PGCE is both economics and business, I signed up for an economics teacher training course." Hull University sounded like a good place to do my teacher training. Rents were much cheaper than around London where I studied for my undergraduate degree. Being a southerner, I also felt the urge for a cultural experience and to head up north. You got chips 'n' gravy with mushy peas in all the chippies, so I was instantly sold.

"The reason you are also being trained for business is that it will help you get jobs in the future. Some schools want both economics and business, so having both will make you more employable." I thought that was why I was also studying french as my subsidiary subject, but what did I know. I was just a raw green recruit into this game of education.

A friend of mine who had previously studied at Hull had tipped me off that it was the only place in the UK where rents were decreasing. I took that as a good sign and had just got on the train and turned up on the day for the course registration. I didn't even have any accommodation pre organised, I just had my backpack. Now that the course registration had been completed, I thought it best to sort out a room for the night, so I headed down the road towards some letting agencies I had noticed earlier. The deal was swiftly done, throw in Sky TV and give me a lift to my new place of abode, and I was ready to sign the contract. This was so much easier than London, where you had to pay months in advance to hold accommodation or just accept resigning yourself to grotty digs. My paltry budget in the past had left me with the latter, so getting accommodation within 10 minutes of needing it was a new and wonderful experience.

I realised that although we were expected to work like professionals, as student teachers we were not being funded like trainee professionals. We were to be funded like students. I could go along with that, if I was to be funded like a student then I would behave like one. My new Norwegian flatmate Harold on the other hand was funded like a king, so my only way to keep up with him was to take on debt. I'd managed to mainly avoid debt on my undergraduate degree by going without, working all holidays, and putting up with less than desirable accommodation. I had only just about managed this because it was back in the tail end era of grants, and before course fees were introduced for university courses. If I had been a student in today's world, I would have graduated owing thousands and thousands of pounds despite working throughout my holidays. It might even have put me off from going to university in the first place. I figured however that after completing my PGCE I'd have a proper job, so I plunged straight into funding my student lifestyle of parties and pubs. Once I got a teaching job, I would be able to pay off my postgraduate debt. This student lifestyle didn't however distract me from my purpose, I took teaching seriously from day one.

St Mary's College Mixed Comprehensive

My first placement was a dreary affair of teaching mainly GCSE economics in the old leaky mobile classrooms at the far end of the playground. My aging mentor quickly taught me not to look too closely at what the pupils were getting up to when crossing the playground to the classroom, that would just lead to writing lots of incident reports. Better to pretend you never saw anything he suggested. The other thing I learnt was that GCSE economics is completely boring, just a list of definitions to memorise with no real understanding or analysis. It was all still invaluable experience, and it helped me get over the trepidation of taking a class for the first ever time. This is a feeling that is hard to explain, a sort of impostor syndrome. You've always been the student and now you are the teacher, and everyone is calling you sir instead of by your name. It would take some time getting used to, but you had to start somewhere, and I had started here.

Bridlington Mixed Comprehensive

To complete the PGCE you had to do some theory essays when based at university and complete 2 teaching placements during the year. The two practical teaching placements were the core of the PGCE course. My 2nd placement would take me to a school on the coast in a town called Bridlington a little to the north of Hull. There were 2 placement schools in Bridlington, and I got the job of driving the Hull University minibus with a dozen or so trainee teachers inside. The steering wheel was huge, the gear stick was tricky, the dimensions of the minibus harder to gauge than the car I was used to, and it lacked acceleration. I nearly clipped the first corner as I drove out of the university but within a few minutes I was getting used to this new beast. The other student teachers had to be picked up and dropped off one by one, but with Oasis and Wonderwall blasting out of the radio we all cheerfully made the round trip each day for the next few months.

The school I had been placed in was set up on a hill overlooking the sea. The pupils gazed longingly out of the huge glass windows dreaming of being deck chair attendants when they grew up. They were mainly disinterested, and my mentor would just sit lazily in his back office, sipping tea whilst I took his lessons. My first mentor in my first placement was a kindly old professor type, my second mentor however was a conceited bully. I remember him doubting my ability to change the OHP bulb, insisting on checking I had managed to do it correctly despite my saying so. When I went for an interview for my first teaching job, he told me not to worry when I didn't get it. I took great satisfaction in informing him later that in fact I had managed to secure my first teaching job. His only response was to say that I hadn't passed my PGCE yet, not congratulations or well done. He was completely pompous and full of his own self-importance. I also remember the school was a split site, which was a bit of a nightmare for the teachers. Break time was often used for driving from one site to the other. As I was teaching french as well as business and economics, I would rush from a first form class where I had been doing a flashcard vocab presentation, to upper sixth debates on the state of the economy and what the correct government response should be. This juxtaposition was not always the easiest and the upper sixth would sometimes wonder why I was still bouncing around instead of being on a calmer more even keel. I realised that teaching french was not my long-term career goal, and that I would just use it to get my foot in the door of schools. My passion was and would always be for teaching economics.

It was also on my second placement that I remember a fellow student teacher called Gareth bursting into the staffroom and declaring that he was in love with a girl from the upper sixth. I sat him down, calmed him down, told him he was in lust and that he needed to get a grip of himself. I think I may have saved his career that day.

Whilst on my PGCE I was selected along with two other students to represent Hull University at an education conference in Paderborn in Germany. We had to leave extremely early in the morning, and I was hosting a house party the night before. It was a recipe for exhaustion. With barely a couple of hours sleep, I made my way to the airport, and later slept on the train as it travelled through Germany. When we arrived in Paderborn, we were each put up by a different member of the university staff in Germany. I'd stayed in French and Belgian families before, but never in a German household. I told the husband of the faculty member I was staying with that although I'd heard German beer was good, my Belgian friends claimed that Belgian beer was better. Goaded in a friendly manner, he took the bait and then spent the entire evening pouring me free German beer from his extensively stocked beer cabinet. I only thought it polite at the end of the evening to say that he'd converted me, and that in fact German beer was better than Belgian beer. It was the least I could do. Educational conferences had a knack of having such fun moments.

I was soon back to Hull where the daily minibus journeys to Bridlington seemed to pass in a flash and come to an end, with the sounds of Wonderwall trailing off into the ether. I told one of the other trainee teachers on the minibus that I was going back down south as I had a job lined up and she made it obvious that had I stayed up north she might have hooked up with me. She wasn't my type. The choices we make and the meandering paths we follow could be so different but for a few words here and there. Still, I had no regrets, I made my farewells to my Norwegian flatmate Harold and all the international students like Torsten from East Germany, Dipa and Jenny from Malaysia, and Carmen from Barcelona that he had introduced me to, and I headed back south towards London. Hull had been fun and was the making of my career, but it was time to move on. New horizons, new experiences and a new chapter awaited me. I was about to start properly my adult life. I was about to become a real and responsible professional teacher. I thought it was time to buy my first mobile phone and to get myself an email account. I would also need a car. Life was getting more serious. I was getting a real job and I needed to act the part.

The Early Years 1996 - 2008

Northwood Hills Mixed Comprehensive

Northwood Hills was an eye opener. Before starting life as a teacher, I had naively believed that everyone wanted to learn and that everyone had the ability if they applied themselves. Tragically some kids are lost. Often, it's down to family background, poor role models and bad choices. Sometimes it may be down to extra obstacles that come their way that they can't overcome. Not everyone is born with a silver spoon in their mouth, in fact very few are. Despite all this Northwood was a great deal of fun. It was here where I truly learnt my craft. I was set loose teaching both A-levels and GCSE classes in both economics and business studies, plus I still had some french teaching. I joined with about a dozen or so other new young teachers, which made all the difference to how we all coped. We bonded as a group, supporting each other at every twist and turn. We both worked hard and played hard. We became like an extended family.

GCSE business studies lessons were always a challenge. They were effectively three lessons in one. Some kids could barely write whilst others were aiming for Oxbridge entry. There were those who wanted to work and those who were determined not to. I was expected to prepare what was in effect three different lessons for each lesson and target my teaching at each individual student according to their needs and abilities. Management called this differentiation. In theory it makes sense but in practice it is just a recipe to break and destroy the teacher. The workload required for all this is an unfair ask and it is no wonder so many teachers leave the profession in the first few years. They realise the loss of work life balance and all the responsibility is not sufficiently financially compensated. They get a job elsewhere that pays better, has less stress, and which requires a fairer amount of work. Personally, I object to poorly behaved students disrupting those who want to learn. I also realised early on that I believed in differentiation by outcome. That means the teacher treats all pupils equally, supplies structure to a course and supplies all the necessary resources to enable everyone a fair chance of passing the exam. Help is always offered to pupils who need it. In the end the pupils who work harder tend to achieve the better results. This only seems fair. Why shouldn't university admissions tutors not be able to differentiate between the hard-working students and the students who put in little effort? In the end not everyone can achieve an A grade, as there needs to be some system to rank students when they apply to university or to a job. Therefore, differentiation by outcome just means different students get different grades, and it is often linked to effort. I completely agree with this, it just seems fair and an effective way to rank student attainment.

Of course, we don't live in a meritocracy, something I learned myself whilst at university. Many of my friends who had gone to private school received poorer grades yet had contacts to open doors for them and went on to greater things despite their general lack of ability. It's the way of the world, and it is considered by them the height of bad manners to suggest that they only got on due to their contacts instead of their own hard work and ability. The truth can sometimes hurt but the system is rigged to perpetuate this inequality which doesn't reward ability and effort but social class instead. Smoke and mirrors and a game of misdirection has been introduced to try and fool many state school students that with hard work they can achieve the best positions in society. Whilst it is not impossible, the cards are stacked up against those from poorer backgrounds. It serves as a useful deflection though to let the general population believe that with hard work and effort they have as much chance as those from more privileged backgrounds. It just isn't true, and many state school kids knew it. Still what else is there to do but play the game, work hard and hope that you end up as one of the lucky ones, the alternative is to just give up which is never a good idea.

There were always distractions. One lesson two of the girls sitting in the front row had the words love and you written onto their eyelids, and they kept blinking at me. I was fast learning the art of not noticing. Another lesson I had to go out and take a phone call in the office whilst I left the rugby lads to quieten down the class thug. Sometimes we had to use the Aussie backpacker substitute teachers to tell off the kids for us, as the permanent staff weren't allowed to properly do so due to the instructions of the overly liberal headmistress. The Aussies though didn't care as they didn't need a reference from a London school when they got back home to Oz. All we had to do was take them down the pub and buy them some free beer and they'd do anything we asked. One Friday evening out in Hammersmith with the Aussies, we all got so hammered that we lost each other in the pub and had to make our own way home on the tube wondering what had happened to each other. We all had a good laugh about that the next time we were in school. I saw and experienced many things at Northwood, it was a steep learning curve, a place where you earned your stripes.

My sixth form once told me that all the best teachers eventually leave Northwood. I didn't believe them, but as is often the case the kids were yet again to be proven right. This wasn't though before one of the students in the class called Monal herself first left. She thought teaching and learning was like a sponge, the teacher poured out the information and performed some magic, and she would then absorb everything with no effort. I warned her but she refused to listen. She failed all her lower sixth end of year exams and was kicked out of the school.

One day a staff member called Mark was waddling down the school corridor glued to a stool, whilst a baying pack of school kids were jeering him as he cried and were throwing paper at him. We were close to the male staff toilets so I told him to go inside and sit down, he couldn't really do much else, and I then tackled the kids and sent for the deputy head teacher. As the NASUWT teacher trade union representative, I later sat in on meetings which discussed his redundancy. The kids broke him, and he quit the profession in the middle of what appeared to me as a mental break down. On a different afternoon one Friday, I went into the staffroom with my friend Steve and saw a young substitute teacher ripping up the teaching planner he had been left by the senior teacher who was on maternity leave. He couldn't cope anymore, he had cracked. He never came back on Monday. He said he was done with teaching. It's not an easy profession, especially in tough schools with poorly behaved pupils.

Another time a kid called Jennings came bursting through one of my classroom doors and bursting out the other whilst hotly being chased by a member of the public. I sent one of the pupils in my class to fetch the management and I promptly chased after them. I found the pupil being held up against a fence by the scruff of his neck in the school carpark by the member of the public. I quickly got in the way and started talking, trying to diffuse the situation. A few minutes later the same deputy head teacher arrived on the scene and took over. It transpired that the pupil worked for the member of the public in his garage repair shop, and he had been stealing from the till. The outcome agreed was that the pupil pay him back with no charges, and the school wouldn't press any charges for trespassing.

We used to race the wheelie chairs around the staff workroom on a Friday afternoon which was quite juvenile, but we got some fun out of it. We'd often then head to the pub next to the local tube station Northwood Hills and spend the entire Friday night there. It's how we kept sane. Some of the other teachers kept sane by smoking in the staff smoking room. They'd tell the kids off for smoking as it was against the school rules, and then they would go and grab a quick ciggie for themselves. All the pupils could see them whenever the staffroom door was opened, but it never stopped them. Schools no longer have staff smoking rooms. I just find it hard to believe that they ever had them in the first place. Then there was the teacher who had responsibility for the under the stage area. One of my best friends Pat had complained to the headmistress about pupils smoking dope, and she was outraged when the headmistress replied she'd have to sack half the staff if she cracked down on cannabis in the school. My friend was Spanish and took this as a personal insult and was fuming. I suggested she vent her frustrations on me, but she'd need to walk and talk. I was going to see Stevo the teacher who controlled the under the stage area in the school. It was the middle of the day. When we arrived my friend Pat was still venting and then her jaw dropped. Stevo was merrily smoking what appeared to be dope right in front of our faces. I then suggested to her that this is what the headmistress was probably talking about.

I tried to get as much involved as possible at Northwood. One December I even volunteered for a charity haircut up on the school stage. All the school piled in to watch my head being shaved to a number one. It was meant to be a number three haircut, but the kids put on the wrong clippers on purpose and gave me a skinhead. The whole school loved it. I couldn't believe how cold my ears were. I also noticed over the next couple of weeks that people avoided me in shops and pubs, serving me quickly so I would go away. They must have thought that because I had a skinhead, I must be violent or something. In the end it was an interesting personal social experiment. The things you get back from giving to charity. You just never know how giving shall rebound in some positive way. Not that I ever wanted to repeat the experiment and become a skinhead again.

Northwood was like an extension of university. We played 5-a-side against the kids and were always giving them asked for advice. One kid called Toby whilst passing in the corridor asked me what he should give his girlfriend for Valentine's Day, so I quickly suggested a plastic rose. It was meant as a joke, I never actually thought for one second that he would take me seriously. Soon afterwards I saw him again and he was a bit upset, so I asked him why. He responded that if I recalled I had suggested he give his girlfriend a plastic rose. My heart nearly stopped, surely not, he couldn't have taken my suggestion seriously. He did though hang on my every word, and he had given her a plastic rose for Valentine's Day and she had swiftly dumped him. An awkward silence followed, before I asked if he had gotten the plastic rose back, to which he replied yes, he had. Ah well then, I offered as I quickly ran off down the corridor, it's not all bad at least you can use the plastic rose again.

Maybe I did him a favour and saved him from a life of arguing, or maybe I ruined a blossoming romance. I shall never know which, but I did learn to be more careful with my words afterwards.

The staff were often worse than the pupils, and the worst of all were the PE staff. Their leader in chief was the head of department Moyley who used to sell second-hand trainers to the kids out of the PE office and who would skip the next day of school if the management ever dared to put him on cover. One day after school I went into the staffroom and the two PE teachers Scarby and Coxy were talking to the headmistress. They were behind the counter by the sink with the tap on, and they could only be seen from the waist up. I went around to make a cup of tea and they were both pissing into the sink whilst talking to the headmistress! It was unbelievable. The management weren't much better, the old female deputy head used to keep a framed photo of my friend Steve, also known as Mr D, on her desk in her office. She was thirty years older than us, fancied him, and was implying that if he wanted to be her special friend, she could help get him promoted. The other male deputy head teacher always had a secret stash of unending wine whenever we had a staff function. Christmas parties and summer BBQs would often end in food fights. The worst was when the PE boys took us to a pub that turned out to be a stripper club. One of the PE boys Scarby ended up on the pool table wearing a toga with a toilet seat around his neck, whilst being whipped by the stripper. At that moment my mum phoned, and Scarby swiped my phone from me and started merrily chatting with my mum. On handing it back my mum asked me where I was, and what was all that noise in the background. I was mortified.

We often as staff went out and socialised together. Sometimes around each other's houses, sometimes clubbing, and sometimes to student parties. It was the wild west. The tequila chili con carne party at my friend Pat's house was one that got messy. The insanity sauce that I used as my secret ingredient was so hot it left me with my mouth under the tap for ten minutes just to cool down, but the evening was really about who could cook the best chili, me, or Patricia? In the end we called it a draw and consumed lots of tequila. I don't like tequila; it doesn't sit well with me. The next day at school was one of the only two times in my 30-year career that I have had a killer hangover. I was feeling so bad that I asked one of the kids to go to the vending machine and get me a bottle of water. Kids know when you're not ok, and they asked if I was alright. They had heard of the staff party and asked if I was hungover. What was I to say? I blamed my friend Pat for food poisoning me instead. It wasn't long afterwards that she found me stating that the kids were having a go at her for poisoning me. I looked at her imploringly, saying I owed her one, and what else could I say? I couldn't admit to being hung over. I realised I should have stayed off work that day. Pat was a good friend, took it on the chin and said I did indeed owe her. This is what I mean by us all looking out for each other. We were like a band of brothers and sisters.

Another time I accidentally took the staff to a pole dancing club. I was again mortified, I thought it was a regular nightclub. On the way back in the van being driven by the head of english, whilst I was eating a hot dog, we went over a bump and the back door of the van flew open wide, and I was suddenly falling head-first out of the van. It could have been the end of me. Lorraine, the girl next to me grabbed me quick and pulled me back in. To this day she doesn't fully remember the incident because she was also drunk at the time, but I remember as it sobered me up. I went on to marry her and have kids. Again, it just shows how life twists and turns on small incidents.

There was also the time at a student party when two girls asked me would I stay over and share their sleeping bags with them. This was a total shock. We never went to student sixth form parties for that, we just went for a few drinks and to chat. I immediately grabbed my friend Steve and told him we were leaving pronto. He could see something was wrong and that now was not the time to ask. He understood and we left as fast as possible. I have never been to a student party since. Times have changed. Back then staff went to student parties, it was normal. What was acceptable in the early years of my career soon became unacceptable as the years progressed. Northwood was a time and a place, in many ways the last of the wild west. Older staff were taking early retirement, ICT was moving on at a rapid pace, and teaching was beginning to rapidly change.

On another note, I also went around my future wife's flat once for a party and noticed painted orange swirls on the walls. As it was the flat of an art teacher it seemed to make sense. In future years I was to see the orange swirls again on the walls of her mum's house back in Belfast.

When I started teaching, we used chalk boards, OHP sheets, and white boards with pens. There was no internet to speak off, no digital resources and digital gradebooks. Everything was photocopied physically, and detention sheets were written out on multi sheet carbon paper. ICT was to change everything, and I caught the last few years and a glimpse of teaching before technology took over. The older teachers used to talk of teaching before the national curriculum when teachers could teach what they liked. They made it sound like some far-off distant teaching utopia that had just vanished one day before their very eyes. It was well before my time in teaching and not anything I ever directly experienced. I could myself though see the appeal of a national curriculum to improve the consistency of teaching, but in truth ever since its implementation the trend has been for an increased workload on teachers and a greater centralisation in decision making in schools. This may be good for managers, but it makes the job of teaching less appealing. It's a trend that has since continued apace over the years.

As teachers we also used to invigilate external exams. You couldn't invigilate exams in your own subject area, but you did invigilate exams in other subjects. One day I was invigilating an A-level french exam, and I was walking up and down the exam hall checking that all was how it should be. Walking past one of the girls from my economics A-level class, I noticed she was answering her A-level french exam incorrectly. French was my subsidiary subject on my PGCE, and I felt my professionalism being put in an awkward position. I should not have been instructed to invigilate an A-level exam in my subsidiary subject whilst my own economics students were sitting it. It pained me, but I took a deep breath and said nothing to the poor girl and walked on. It was all I could do whilst maintaining my professionalism. It would have been so easy to have whispered the answer into her ear, but I didn't. I remember thinking that teachers should not be placed in such situations and should not be invigilating external exams. Later in my career when I was in Northern Ireland this was the case. Schools in Northern Ireland employ external invigilators and do not allow the teachers to invigilate. This seems to me to be a much better system.

There was still a snobbery over academic courses back then. The vocational GNVQ courses were soon nicknamed Going Nowhere Very Quickly, or Generally Not Very Well Qualified. It is a problem with education. The schools were funded to teach academic courses and would need new funding to set up vocational courses. Funding which the government clearly wasn't prepared to supply. This meant some kids who would have been better off on truly vocational courses were stuck with academic courses. They were like square pegs in a round hole. This attributed to their poor behaviour but no one in authority truly cared. After all, teaching to the powers that be of state school kids was more about providing child-care so the parents could go out to work. Actual education was more for the kids of the well off. GNVQs were a semi-academic attempt at vocational courses. No wonder they never truly took off. What was needed was technical colleges like they have in Germany which I witnessed first-hand during my PGCE on an education conference at Siemens

Nixdorf in Paderborn, but what we had instead was comprehensives that lacked the equipment to be able to teach vocational courses effectively.

Report writing came with rules. We'd often use statement banks and tweak them for he and she, and for weak, average, and strong students. You'd then try to personalise them to some extent. Report writing and marking are the two most disliked duties of teachers. However, with reports you could only write positive comments. There was one report that I had to take to the head of year for some advice. The pupil was poorly behaved, did little work and barely attended school. It was getting towards the end of fifth form, and she would soon be leaving the school. All I could find to write was that she had been on the school roll for 5 years, and that the school wished her every success in the future. The head of year Raymondo looked at me, looked at the name of the pupil, read my sentence and said he understood my problem and would be taking it to show to the deputy head teacher. In the end the report remained as I had written it. It is rare but there are times when you struggle to be able to write anything positive. I always tell the pupils that they in effect write their own reports, so the girl in the end had no one else to blame but herself. Zoe just wanted to leave school and become a hairdresser. Her dad was a policeman and didn't know what to do with her himself, she was out of control.

During a parent's evening one time I had to sit back as the divorced parents started bickering amongst themselves. My poor student was horrified. Her parents were embarrassing her in front of her teacher. I couldn't intervene and stop them from arguing, it wasn't my place. The poor girl snapped, told them both off, and then looked at me imploringly. I took the lead and moved the conversation on. It's no wonder the pupils behave the way they do sometimes. As teachers we don't know half the baggage that they bring into the classroom from their home life. It's one reason I always try to be pleasant to my students. In my classroom they know it's a safe, secure, and friendly environment, where the learning is organised and structured. They know that I care. I think this is the secret to my success in teaching.

In amongst all of this I used to go down twice a week to the hammersmith hospital where my older brother was when he was receiving treatment for his leukaemia. The hospital staff were wonderful and did everything they possibly could. My big brother Andrew eventually died but the NHS staff deserve medals for all the good work they do for the rest of us. I still miss Andrew to this very day; he was our commander in chief as kids and I'd have to continue without him. It was a huge loss that hit me hard, that I still carry around with me today.

I took the spare boy's football team one year. The PE staff needed someone to take one of the teams, so I volunteered. I spoke to the boys and let them organise themselves. We played a flat 4-4-2 with the strongest players in central positions. We had a strong core to the team. I had to referee home games and would get dog's abuse from angry parents. As the season went on it all came down to the last game. If we were to win the last game, we would get promoted. The only problem was that it was away against by far the best team in the league. We headed off with little hope. The rules stated that the home team had to provide the referee or forfeit the match. When we arrived their PE teacher wasn't there, they had no referee. They asked me to ref but ever the strategist I refused. My team wanted to play, and they started to complain, I quickly told them to be quiet. After the official time limit was up, and not having provided a ref, the home team forfeited the match. We were promoted. We quickly got back onto our bus, but not quickly enough. A mob was forming outside the school and as we drove out bricks flew through our windows. Fortunately, no one was hurt. We arrived back to Northwood where I informed Moyley the head of PE what had happened. All he cared about was the result, I'd gotten the spare team promoted. He made me manager of the month and toasted my success. Although my boys had wanted to play, they were happy in the end. They were champions. We were winners. We had all been successful, albeit with some opportunistic twists and turns along the way.

Shortly before my leaving Northwood, a game of rounders was organised between the staff and the pupils. I hesitated to play and then decided against it. On the day itself the staff were one person short of a team, so they twisted my arm and I agreed to play. I only had my suit with me, so I took off my jacket and headed off to the fields. It was a close game, and it came down to me making base for the win for the staff. The only problem was that I was not going to make it. It was quite wet underfoot, so I made an instant decision. Launching myself through the air I landed on the ground, lifted my legs, and aquaplaned to victory and glory. I made base just and the staff won the game. On standing up my entire trousers, shirt and tie were covered in mud. After several washes I had to give up on the shirt and tie and just bin them. At least my trousers were salvaged. Northwood was like that, full of crazy fun moments, but also full of many tough moments trying to get the pupils to behave and focus. It was one of those places where you thought you would stay forever but after four years I decided to move on and see what other jobs in other schools I could find. Sometimes you just know when it's the right time to move on, and you need to listen to your instincts.

On my leaving day at the end of term summer BBQ, my friends gave me a harmonica that I still play around with today. I gave my leaving speech, thanking them all for all the support and fun times. It was very emotional and felt like I was leaving my family, which in some ways I was. I'd been on a one hundred day count down and was feeling a little bit worse for the wear, but I still noticed people weren't really paying attention. Then one of my friends called out saying that they all just wanted to know why I had a quiver slung over my back. Smiling, I reached over my shoulder, unzipped the top of my cooler bag, and pulled out a nice cold can of beer, which I promptly opened and started to drink. There was a cheer, and as the day drew on, I felt some sense of sadness. All my friends for so long would no longer be part of my daily life. We would always stay friends but it's never the same when you are no longer rubbing shoulders on a day-to-day basis. Over the years our times together at Northwood would fade into memories, but for just that moment in time we were all very close. That's both the magic and sadness of life, nothing lasts forever but, in that moment special magic can be made. Steve, Pat, and the gang were the perfect start to my teaching career and shall stay with me forever. That night after the leaving party, I went out with my future wife Lorraine into London for some drinks, and I at least managed to hold on to the most important person I met whilst at Northwood. For that I am thankful.

Years after I left Northwood, they knocked the old school building down and built a new state of the art school building in its place. They bulldozed my memories for the sake of progress. I'm sure today's pupils are better served by the new school building, so I can happily live with that.

Northern Ireland 2000

After leaving Northwood I took the summer off before heading over to Northern Ireland to visit my now girlfriend in Belfast during August. It went well so I decided to move over permanently in October. I packed my car and headed north again, taking a slight detour enroute to have a look at Hadrian's Wall. I stayed overnight in a B&B in Stranraer, where I took in a documentary on The Battle of Hastings on TV. I caught the ferry the next morning from Scotland to Northern Ireland.

The peace process had not long been signed. Helicopters still hovered over the city, lamp posts were still painted red, white, and blue in the part of town I was heading to, and the union flag was still flying over the city hall. Taking out the yellow pages I wrote a letter to every school in the city hoping to get some substitute teaching. Unlike in England, Northern Irish schools didn't use recruitment agencies. You needed to contact them directly. I was feeling confident as my girlfriend had told me there was a national UK teacher shortage. Little did I know that this didn't include Northern Ireland which has a teacher surplus. It has its own teacher training college called Stranmillis that churns out teachers for the UK, but who then mainly only want to stay and work in Northern Ireland. Many want to stay near their mummies, and don't want to work away across the water on the mainland in England. This causes such a glut of teachers in Northern Ireland and some newly qualified teachers only ever become classroom assistants, whilst others never even get started on a teaching career before giving up and leaving the profession. Still, I was born lucky in many ways. Of course, in life you often make your own luck to an extent, but you still need a break. My four years of essential experience at Northwood must have set me apart from all the newly qualified teachers from Stranmillis who lacked any real experience.

Larne Grammar School Mixed Grammar

I managed to get a few days' supply teaching in my girlfriend's new school. It was a lovely quiet country grammar school. Northern Ireland is different from England. There isn't a private school sector where parents must pay astronomical fees. Instead, there are state grammar schools. Some are single gender, some are mixed gender schools, but they all have an ethos of hard work and academic achievement. I went to an all-boys grammar school myself in Gloucester when I was growing up, so I was perfectly at home with the Northern Irish education system. In many ways I preferred it to the system in England.

Whilst talking about Northern Ireland, house prices are also much more reasonable. The people are friendly and welcoming. Provided you can get a job the living standards for normal people are much better in Northern Ireland than the South of England where teachers can't afford to buy a decent house anymore.

At Larne Grammar they gave me history classes to cover. I love history. I love history so much that I refused to take it at school for O-level because they didn't cover the specific period of history I was most interested in back then. I wanted to study Roman History, not 20th century European History. As luck would have it the lesson I was covering was on The Battle of Hastings and The Norman Conquest. I'd only just been watching that in Stranraer in Scotland when I'd been waiting to get the ferry over to Belfast. So instead of just baby-sitting the class, I got up and taught them. The senior cover teacher looked through the classroom door amazed that I was teaching history when I was an economics and business studies teacher. As I said, I was born lucky in many ways. I only worked a few days in Larne, enough to see it was a lovely school, but I needed to find myself another more permanent job.

Carrickfergus College Mixed Comprehensive

I got a call and did several days at Carrickfergus College. This was a tough mixed comprehensive school. On my first day before I even walked into a classroom, I learnt the names of all the head of years. These kids were waiting to eat substitute teachers alive, but my four years teaching in the London comprehensive had given me the necessary experience to see what was coming. In these situations, you need to borrow the authority of the head of year first before you can then start to exert your own authority. As soon as the pupils started to try it on, I sent immediately for the ball crushing head of year. He roasted them alive and afterwards the kids did as I said. Too many new teachers believe they must cope on their own. They try to be best friends with the students and to try and contain bad behaviour as they see asking for help as failing. It is one of the biggest and most common mistakes in teaching. I know, because I made the same mistake myself for a while at the start of my own career. I can't say I got too much job satisfaction out of working in this type of school. All schools are different, and all teachers are different. The trick is to understand yourself, and to then find a school that matches what you are looking for. If you take a job in the wrong type of school for you, then it won't work out so well in the end. I was beginning to understand that I liked working in more academic schools. Perhaps this was because I went to a grammar school myself and this was what I knew and understood myself best.

Bloomfield Collegiate All Girls Grammar

As fortune would have it after only a couple of weeks in Belfast an advert in the paper appeared for a job teaching economics and business studies in an all-girls grammar school. It was the end of October, most teachers were set up for the year, but I had just got off the boat just as the perfect job came up. Job shortage in Belfast for teachers, what job shortage? I still don't appreciate just how lucky I was. Call it fate perhaps but it couldn't have been planned any better. It was only a job covering a maternity until the following summer, but that's all I needed at that precise moment. It would give me an invaluable local reference, and label me as a grammar-school teacher. One door leads to another, and my year at Bloomfield Collegiate set me on the path in Northern Ireland. We called Bloomfield the Pink Palace. We only just had enough men for a 5-a-side team. We had to play teachers from other schools as we didn't have enough ourselves for a match. The men in Bloomfield were treated so well. All the female staff and all the girls were extremely nice to us. We were such a rarity in the school that it felt like they were so glad to have us. The girls worked so hard in class. There were no boys to distract them, and they were all keen to do well. It was such a lovely year and it helped me enormously to settle into Northern Ireland. I was sorry when my time was up. If I had girls myself, I would send them to an all-girls grammar school without hesitation. My wife went to an all-girls grammar school though when she was younger and says I didn't see all-girls schools through the same lens as her. I still maintain that I think all-girls schools are better for girls, and whilst mentioning it I think boys are better in mixed schools. The girls help to calm the boys down. One of the male teachers called Paul at Bloomfield went on to be my wife's vice principal at Larne Grammar School. Northern Ireland is a small world. Fortunately for me I was brought up in a village, so this suits me well.

Castlereigh Mixed FE College

Whilst working at Bloomfield I also started working at Castlereigh Further Education College where I taught A-level business studies to adult night classes once a week. Teaching adults is completely different to teaching kids. The adults want to learn and concentrate harder, allowing you to get through more content in a lesson. They however often struggle more with exams as they are not so well drilled in writing exam answers. It was another new experience. The problem though was the lack of time. An A-level course is meant to take 2 years; Castlereigh College was delivering an A-level course in one 2-hour lesson a week for nine months. I started in October and the previous teacher had not made a good start to the class, so I even had less time. Some of the adults dropped away but those that remained saw it through to the end. By the time of the exam, they at least had covered the course and had seen past papers and mark schemes. It required them to do a lot of reading outside of class each week. Some of them managed to pass and get an A-level, which all things considered was a good achievement. One of the adult learners was a businessman and he even hired me to go into his company for a few sessions and help train his staff. I took this as a positive endorsement of my teaching.

By the time the maternity cover at Bloomfield had finished, I had managed to get a full-time permanent job at another grammar school in Northern Ireland. With a new permanent job, I decided I no longer needed to continue teaching adult night classes as well. Getting a permanent job also allowed me to get a mortgage and buy a house with my girlfriend, who had now become my fiancée. This was something I could only ever have dreamed of back in London where house prices were astronomical. Wallace High School was a mixed grammar school in Lisburn, a town a few miles outside of Belfast. It was handy on either the train or by driving, and over my time at Wallace I did both. Driving to work is always great for listening to the radio, whilst the train is often good for reading. Luckily, I enjoy both.

Wallace High School Mixed Grammar

I was still teaching french at Wallace as well as economics and business. This would be the last school where I had to teach french, and I'm glad I eventually could just focus on teaching my main subjects. Still, it had its' advantages. I could photocopy my business and economics worksheets on the language department photocopying budget, and I could disappear from the economics department and hide in the languages office if I ever felt like it. The head of languages Pamela became a good friend. She was managing a department of 12 teachers, some part-time, some full-time, but all of them except for me were women. As I was mainly in another department, I wasn't really involved in the politics of the modern foreign languages department. This allowed Pam the head of department to confide in me and gave her someone she could just openly talk to. It was also beneficial because it meant I got on the school trip to Normandy and Paris every year. The trip required three members of staff and at least one man. The head of languages Pam always went and as the only man on the staff who spoke french, she also always took me. The third place rotated but we often took the french teacher Margaret who also happened to be my head of year and who was a great laugh. Teaching french had some advantages.

We always went to Disneyland with the kids, and took them to central Paris, and then on to Normandy. One year the hotel in Paris flooded, and I had to take the boys to another hotel. At that point Pam the head of languages said this was why she always took me, because when the emergency happened, I could step up and be trusted to be able to do what was required. Most of the time I just got her cups of coffee when she looked stressed, but when needed I could be relied upon. Another year the third member of staff Margaret disappeared for a couple of days, and we told the kids she was ill in the hotel room. She left the back of the group in the Musee D'Orsay and got the train back to London. Her brother was a famous Northern Irish celebrity, and she was going as a surprise to his big birthday bash. Margaret got back from London just in time to emerge from her hotel room for the trip back home to Northern Ireland. The kids were none the wiser, they just thought she had been ill the whole time. Normandy was also very interesting. We always went to the cemetery which appears in the film Saving Private Ryan. The kids were always quiet and sombre, and wandered around with deep respect. The symmetry of the crosses in the cemetery made a huge lasting impression on me. Regardless of which direction you looked from, they were always in perfect lines which added to the great sense of the loss of life on D-Day back in June 1944. We would also go down to the local town Arromanches, where one year the kids started talking to old war veterans who were over for a D-Day remembrance service. This was such a joy to witness. The veterans were happy to converse with the kids and it felt like that is why they fought in the war, so that future generations could enjoy more peaceful times.

Wallace was a very traditional academic grammar school, and very protestant. I was still teaching with a chalk board, and if I used red, white, and blue coloured chalk to draw the diagrams in economics then the pupils were very happy. As an experiment once I used white, then green and orange. There was a deathly silence before one of the lads called Simon said I couldn't do that. As an Englishman I feigned ignorance which they accepted, but now that things had been explained to me then I'd better not do it again. I was getting a lesson in Northern Ireland. Simon then gave me a couple of free tickets to go and see Northern Ireland play football at Windsor Park. He wanted to educate me in the ways of NI.

At Christmas the teachers would put on a small sketch in the school Christmas play. When one teacher strode onto the stage in a bowler hat and orange sash, proclaiming "No Surrender" I was flabbergasted. When I mentioned it to other staff, they just brushed it off. Oh, that's just Dickie, he's a member of the Orange Order so it's ok. I liked Dickie. He was an old timer and had a sharp sense of humour. He was a history teacher with a strong sense of his own identity. I dislike Mrs Thatcher for increasing individualism, harming community spirit, and for making the country more selfish. Dickie however loved her for putting as he called it the great back into Great Britain. We agreed to disagree as he acknowledged I was talking from an English perspective whilst he was talking from a Northern Irish one. At the end of the day, they viewed me as a Brit, so they thought I was ok. Welcome again to Northern Ireland.

For my small part in the Christmas play I took on the role of one of the seven dwarfs. We had to shuffle across the stage on our knees. It was agony. The things you do for the kids and the school community. It was all good fun though and worth it.

Wallace had a snooker table in the staff room. I grew up with a snooker table in my bedroom. I watched Alex Higgins win his second World Snooker Championship in the early 1980s with my dad on TV. I watched Dennis Taylor win; I watched Jimmy White lose. I have always been a snooker fan. Every lunchtime I would play snooker in the staffroom with the other guys like Stephen, Richard, and David. Sometimes you had to wait a bit for a game, but you nearly always got a game. The competition was fierce, but it was always a bit of fun. I won the staff tournament one year, and when I left, I bequeathed my friends at Wallace the snooker cue and case that my dad had bought me for my thirteenth birthday. In some ways I regret that, but in others it makes me feel that my spirit lives on in the Wallace staffroom.

Staffrooms are a strange beast. Teachers have their own seats and own mugs, and you'd better obey these rules as a new member of staff, or you shall soon be put in your place. Most people kept to the same corners of the staffroom, but I wanted to get to know as many staff as possible. Before school I would sit in one spot, at break time I would sit more with the girls like Gillian, Julie, Kerry, and Tona, and at lunch time I would mainly play snooker or sometimes sit with the old boys Dickie and Howard. I soon got to know just about all the staff at Wallace, and for the first time since leaving Northwood I felt as if I had found a family again. This has only ever happened in three schools for me, Northwood, Wallace, and later at ACS. These are the special schools where you leave a bit of your soul behind when you depart. The places that you think will never end, yet somehow, they always do.

As an effort to get to know the staff better, I organised some Belfast pub crawls. It was good research for when friends from England came over to visit. I got to know all the traditional bars and all the trendy wine bars. Belfast it must be said is full of great bars. There was much fun and laughter whilst I was at Wallace. However, the day after the night before can be extremely perilous. The time I just made it to the staff toilet at the bottom of the sixth form centre before being violently sick was a case in hand. If I had been any slower and had been sick in front of the students due to a hangover, then I probably would have been sacked. I sailed close to the wind at times but just managed to get away with it. I played hard, but I never forgot to work hard and get good A-level and GCSE results.

There were also the school formals. It's a tradition in Northern Ireland for the upper sixth to hire out a hotel venue for a meal and a dance, and to dress up in formal dress. It was black tie for the boys and lavish dresses for the girls. Many of the staff, including management would attend. Some of the upper sixth would still only be seventeen but that was ignored and there would be a bar for everyone. That has since changed, and schools have tried to distance themselves by saying the formals are not school events, but events organised by the students. Staff were no longer encouraged to attend. Newspapers however still labelled them as school events so in the end the formals could no longer serve drink. Again, times change, but before they did all the staff and students had great times at the formals. I'm sure that many past pupils when looking back on their school years, would pinpoint the formal as one of the major highlights of school. It's a shame that the formals couldn't continue as they had done previously over the many years. It feels like another school tradition has been attacked and diminished due to the relentless march of rules and regulations. At least formals survived in a limited format.

We also would be taken out by our upper sixth classes the last weekend before they left school for their A-level study leave. One year was strange because it was just after the smoking ban was introduced. I don't smoke, but the students mainly disappeared outside the pub to carry on smoking. As I'd been in pubs for years with people smoking it was a bit strange at first, however I do quite like the fact that smoking is not allowed anymore in pubs and restaurants. Then again as a non-smoker I would say that. I used to hate waking up in the morning with my clothes stinking of other people's smoke. Another year I was refused entry into the pub because I was wearing trainers and I had to quickly go home and change whilst all my students were waiting for me. However, the night that most sticks in my memory is the one where they gave me a blue aftershock. I am used to drinking Guinness, and maybe a whiskey chaser at the end of the evening, I had no idea what this drink was. As it went down and hit my stomach, I instantly knew it was not good stuff, my insides were on fire, and it felt like my stomach lining had been stripped away. It didn't agree with me, and I learnt another lesson that night, not to drink anything that you don't know exactly what it is. One of the girls in the class then started flirting with me. By this time, I was married. I didn't expect this in a public place surrounded by all her classmates. I am less forward than this, seeing as I'm from a village, so it took me by surprise. She was one of my students and that is just not right. I had to again retreat from the situation. It was the last time I ever went out with my sixth form. I was a slow learner, but I was learning.

Whilst at Wallace I decided to try out an experiment that I called zonal marking. GCSE business studies coursework is often very descriptive, lacking the amount of analysis and evaluation required for A-level courses. Often the students who put in the most effort obtained the best coursework grades, meaning they had often written the most pages when answering the coursework. Scripts with more pages tend to be heavier than scripts with fewer pages. Before marking the coursework's accurately with the mark schemes, I decided to see if there was a correlation between the number of pages written and the final mark awarded. I marked out different zones on my stairs, with the higher grades at the bottom of the stairs marked out and with the lower grades at the top of the stairs. The idea being that heavier coursework's would fall further once tossed, than lighter coursework's containing fewer pages. I practiced a few tosses first to try and improve consistency in my experiment, and then I started to see which zone all the coursework's would fall into on my stairs. Sure enough, the lighter pieces of coursework with fewer pages fell nearer the top into zones marked with lower grades, and the heavier pieces of coursework fell into lower down zones on my stairs which were marked as higher-grade areas. I noted down all the results, and then collected in all the coursework's to then mark them properly. Once I had marked them all using the exam board mark schemes. I compared the official scores against the scores from my zonal marking experiment.

Surprise! Surprise! There was a high degree of correlation. The pieces of coursework which had scored poorly had mainly landed near the top of the stairs, and those which had scored well after having been marked officially had landed in my experiment near the bottom of my stairs. It seemed indeed that at GCSE at least, which is more descriptive and less analytical than A-levels, there was a large link between the actual score achieved and the amount of effort put in. I may not be the greatest scientist the world had ever seen, but I was surely onto something. I was on to something that all teachers already knew, something that parents knew, that students knew, and that management knew. The results, especially at GCSE, are more about how much work the student puts in. When they performed well, they should be congratulated, but when they didn't do well it was often down to their own lack of effort. It was often not the fault of the teacher. Students own their own results, whether they are good, bad, or indifferent.

In later years I have noticed that more students are suffering from anxiety. I have much more empathy for students suffering with anxiety, than for students who are both lazy and disorganised. Sometimes poor exam results can be due to stress rather than laziness. Coursework can help take away from the stress of final exams for those prepared to put in the effort. For this reason, I used to be all for coursework. Back then coursework couldn't be completed by artificial intelligence, and many kids did most of their own coursework. That would change over the years, which these days brings into question the validity of coursework continuing as an appropriate means of pupil assessment.

The school was really into rugby. One boy who represented Northern Ireland under 18s at football was invisible, but the captain of the school rugby team was a celebrity. Whilst I was there the school won the Northern Ireland cricket and hockey tournaments, but the school really wanted to win the rugby school's cup. Then one year the school made it all the way to the St. Patrick's Day final at Ravenhill. The school went mad. Coachloads of school supporters were bused to the ground, with their faces painted with the school colours of blue and white. We were playing INST, one of the big 3 Belfast schools who dominated the competition over the years. My youngest brother- in-law was on the INST team, and my in-laws were appalled that I was supporting my own school over wee Petey Poos, my baby brother-in-law. INST were favourites but at half time Wallace were winning. Wallace played a narrow game through their pack and the forwards, but at Ravenhill which was a larger pitch this was a more difficult way in which to try and win. According to my brother-in-law, at half-time the INST coach read them the riot act, and in the second half INST came out, played through their backs, and scored a couple of tries to secure the victory. There's a photo of my brother-in-law receiving his winners medal from Prince Andrew, or there used to be at least now that Prince Andrew is disgraced. Wallace was gutted at losing that final, and to this day has still never won the rugby School's Cup. The captain of Wallace Chris Henry went on to play for Ireland in the Six Nations and had a very successful professional rugby career. For the majority however that was the pinnacle of their rugby playing days, and years later when I bumped into Big G in the city centre, we were still talking about it.

When Ireland played England in the 6 Nations at rugby, that was a different story. The first time Ireland beat England whilst I was at Wallace the entire school went mad. They were calling out for me in assembly, and the head of maths ran up to me pumping his fist in my face. Now I don't mind banter, but this was too much. The Celtic dislike of the English was resurfacing, and it was an ugly sight. I told the head of maths to back off or I'd report him for racism. I didn't care about the rugby result, but I did care about harassment. When you are the lone Englishman, you can't take on the whole school. My in-laws are just as bad as they want anyone but England to win at rugby. It is indoctrinated into them from birth. I no longer follow rugby. I no longer want to be subjected to such behaviour. I mainly follow tennis which is less about nationality and more about the individual.

Then Northern Ireland beat England 1-0 at football. Not that it mattered as England still qualified top of the group and Northern Ireland didn't qualify. We had beaten them earlier 4-0 but they liked to forget about that. They still go on about it in Northern Ireland, and I started to get less interested in football as well. I just do not want to be subjected to it. I still always support British teams in the World Cup, so after England I now support Northern Ireland above Scotland and Wales. It is a small sign that Belfast after many years has become my home, as I now rank supporting Northern Ireland second only to England in international football. I must admit that I have a soft spot for The Republic of Ireland as well.

Sometimes however I think my wife has the right idea. She has no interest in either sport or politics and remains blissfully ignorant on such matters.

I also ended up teaching careers whilst I was at Wallace. I've ended up teaching many subjects throughout my career, whilst always teaching my core subjects of economics and business. All schools have different timetabling needs, and it seems I end up helping tie up the loose ends. Not that I teach other subjects to A-level, but still I've proven flexible. To try and name them all, I've taught economics, business, french, maths, geography, history, biology, chemistry, physics, politics, accountancy, ICT, careers, learning for life and work citizenship, learning for life and work employability, travel and tourism, health and social care, design and technology, global studies, and office communication systems. I make that twenty. Twenty subjects and twenty-six schools, a bit more experience than you gain at teacher training.

Careers was mainly about providing students with information, but you also got to take the pupils to the university open days. The best one was Queen's University Belfast. The teachers were treated to a lovely meal in the large wooden panelled hall. You sometimes even got a glass of wine to help with the coach journey back to school.

We also organised work experience for the pupils. During the work experience placement, we'd go out and visit to check that everything was fine. I visited many work placements, of which one of them was Fleming Fulton a special school. Fleming Fulton teaches students with severe special needs, the sort of students that can't be taught in mainstream schools. There were disabled pupils for example who were bed bound. After speaking to the staff, I had nothing but admiration for them. I had spent my career working in mainstream schools, I could not have done the job they were doing. I can do nothing but applaud them, they perform miracles.

Getting involved in extra-curricular clubs and societies is always encouraged in schools. Some schools even insist that staff get involved. At Wallace I used to run the chess club. I organised an internal ladder where students could challenge each other to take the top positions on the ladder. I entered students into the UK chess challenge, where several students often qualified out of the Northern Ireland competition to play at the UK nationals. On open mornings I would get out my three-player chess set and install it in the library as a novelty. Three player chess catches people's attention, but it is confusing to understand how the middle of the board works. It is not actually a game of strategy, but more one of politics. If two players gang up on the third, then even the greatest chess player in the world will lose. It's a bit of trivial fun, but I found it to be useful in promoting school chess clubs.

In my final year at Wallace, I entered the All-Ireland Mock United Nations competition or MUN for short. Grammar schools love to win big trophies, but they were most surprised when we came back as winners. I had researched and drilled my team on the Russian Federation, and they had performed just as I had instructed them to. To this day it's probably the competition I have been the proudest of winning with a school team.

Whilst I was at Wallace my two boys Robbie and Jamie were born. I was now married with a family. I can't imagine a life without my two boys, they are along with Lorraine my wife the making of me. This added responsibility made my final departure from Wallace even more difficult. As did the fact that my dad was dying of lung cancer just as I was leaving.

One afternoon in an after school meeting the headmistress was going through announcements which as mainly sixth form teachers in economics and business, we were paying little attention to. Then she moved on to something called The Entitlement Framework. Little did I know what a major impact this was to have on my life and my family. The Entitlement Framework in essence was a cost cutting exercise. Our school was only going to teach either business studies or economics, and the neighbouring school called Friends a few hundred metres down the road would do the same. This meant that each school could axe an economics / business teacher, save on their budget, and send students to each other's schools for lessons in the subject they had axed. I immediately sat bolt upright. They would not be axing Karen the head of department. Even though I had just been awarded a performance pay rise, I knew my neck was on the chopping block. From that point on I was a dead man walking at Wallace, and it had a dreadful effect on me. It looked like I would have one more year until the arrangements for The Entitlement Framework could be made.

Economics and business teachers have the disadvantage that their subject is not taught throughout the school to every year group. English, maths, and sciences for example could not be axed as easily as they are core subjects rather than optional subjects only at GCSE and A-level.

I realised I was being set up for the chop. My timetable fell neatly into the frees of my colleagues Karen and Oonagh. I started showing David Brent from the BBC show The Office to my GCSE business studies class to demonstrate poor leadership. I was on a downhill spiral. I should have waited it out for a redundancy payment, but I became too hot headed, and I left the school in January. I didn't tell anyone at the school except the headmistress. One day I was there, then suddenly, I wasn't. Leaving a school like this is never a good idea in the long run. It had a huge impact on my mental health. I lost all my friends of the last seven years, and it was as if the last seven years hadn't happened. My confidence hit a low. My career was torpedoed, and in Northern Ireland where finding a permanent teaching job was extremely difficult, I was in a lot of trouble. Having climbed the pay scale and being more expensive than beginning teachers made it even harder, as did not being a local with plenty of contacts. I had a mortgage to pay, and a young family to help support and things did not look rosy. On later reflection I decided never to leave a school in such a way again. Another time I would instead either stay and tough it out for a redundancy pay-out, or I would leave properly by saying goodbye openly to everyone and leaving with my mental health intact. This however didn't help me at the time. I needed a new job, and I needed one quickly. Throughout all this my dad was also dying of lung cancer which added to my sense of despair. My dad was my hero, and I was in shock at the prospect of losing him. He would have been a wonderful grandfather to both Robbie and Jamie and is such a huge loss that they can't ever truly understand. Andrew my older brother may have been our commander in chief as kids, but my dad was our true leader. My childhood family had been decimated before our time.

Through this difficult time my wife stood by me and reminded me that I was a professional teacher. She quickly helped get me back up on my feet, and I very quickly started to look for substitute teaching. If you fall off the horse the best therapy often is to get back on as quickly as possible. Whatever comes your way you need to pick yourself up and carry on. My nan taught me this, she was part of the generation that went through the second world war. I stared into the abyss and came out the other side stronger. It was a life changing experience.

Up until this point in my career I had been getting myself firstly established in teaching, and then established in Northern Ireland. From this point I started to go on my travels. Without The Entitlement Framework I would probably have spent my entire career at Wallace. Although my career has been less secure and less stable, it has been far more enriching. It was never planned but circumstances forced me to go on my travels so to speak. I have experienced far more schools because of this and have met far more teachers and students. It has given me such a wider experience and understanding of education and of life. I would have played it safe, especially with the responsibility of a young family, but if you get lucky life can be more rewarding if you take chances. Not only have I taught many subjects, but I have taught in many types of schools. All-girls grammar, all-boys grammar, mixed grammar, mixed comprehensive, further education college, integrated school, catholic school, mixed secondary, brethren school, all-boys private school, international college, international private school with boarding. Every school was different, and in each I learnt new lessons.

After thirteen years of teaching, I was back to writing letters to schools looking for supply work. My next five years would be a string of short term and one-year contracts, and then it would take me many years to get back to the same position that I had been in at Wallace. That is, an established permanent member of staff. The Entitlement Framework had the one single biggest impact upon all my years of teaching. It set me upon a path I could never have predicted. Not that I'd ever actually predicted going to Northern Ireland either.

The Middle Years 2008 - 2012

Carrickfergus Mixed Grammar

The first school to respond to my cold letters was Carrickfergus Grammar. Out of all the grammars I have been to in Northern Ireland, this is the one that felt most like a comprehensive. There was a long tail of under achieving boys, some of whom also had poor behaviour. I was grateful for the work, and it helped me get back into the classroom as quickly as possible, but it isn't the school in which I've been that I have most enjoyed. The staff were fine, but there was a slight atmosphere which undermined academic effort.

Malone Integrated College Mixed Comprehensive

Malone Integrated College was also contacting me about doing some supply work. They wanted me to cover business studies lessons for a member of staff off on the sick. I found this school much more interesting. It was not a grammar school but was one of the few integrated schools in Northern Ireland. This means, a school where both Protestants and Catholics go to school together. At the interview they asked me what I thought about integrated education. As an Englishman religion growing up was not an issue. I had friends for many years before finding out they were Catholics, and when I did it was just some unimportant part of some forgotten and insignificant conversation. We just didn't do religion growing up, we were post-religion. Therefore, when asked I just replied that I didn't think anything about integrated education except that it was normal. I guess that response was more than they anticipated in Northern Ireland, and they decided I was the man for the job. The kids and staff were friendly enough and my brief time at Malone Integrated College was fine. I did notice that on the bell at the end of the school day the Catholic kids went to the right heading to The Fall's Road, whilst the Protestant kids turned left heading towards Finaghy. In school they talked about different corner shops and different chip shops. They brushed shoulders in school, and all got on fine, but outside of school they were still segregated living different lives. I guess it is a start, as otherwise some of these kids might have grown up without ever meeting anyone from the other side so to speak. I realised myself that I only knew the Finaghy area and knew nothing about The

Fall's Road and West Belfast. I had grown up watching images on national TV and had felt it was a no-go area. Determined to understand my pupils a bit better, one night I got in my car and drove around The Falls Road. It was only an extra five minutes' drive from places I had known for years. The thing is, Belfast is only a small city. In many ways it's like a big village. There are places almost right next to each other that people from the other community never venture into. From talking to my father-in-law, Belfast has changed for the better and come on hugely since the peace process. However, it is still not completely normalised, and the peace still needs to be nurtured. With that said the vast majority from all sides do not support violence and never have. It's always only been a small minority. After driving around West Belfast I did get to understand my Catholic pupils a bit better. Integrated education is an important step in the right direction for Northern Ireland, although a fully integrated education system does not look likely in any foreseeable future. It is still years if not decades off by my reading.

Dundonald High School Mixed Comprehensive

I then did a few weeks work in Dundonald High School. This was the most depressing school I have ever worked in. The student roll was dropping, and the school had the shadow of closure hanging over it. There were mini staff rooms, and this made the staff fragmented. You sat at break time with only a couple of colleagues who taught in the nearby classrooms. Despite this the kids remained somewhat upbeat. They adjusted to their surroundings and just got on with things. One of the staff asked me what was I doing at Dundonald, didn't I know they were being closed? The staff were depressed. I have never met depressed staff before; it was a sad sight to see. Teachers always moan about workload, large classes, autocratic management, but underneath it all they are still motivated to help and do their best for the pupils. At Dundonald, for the first and only time in my career I encountered staff who had been beaten into submission and who were defeated. They were just waiting to be axed. The buildings were in a state of disrepair and there was a sense of decay hanging about. Dundonald High School still exists today; it was not closed. I don't know the precise details but it unlike some other schools got a stay of execution. I think it was the only main school in the immediate area, and the parents helped to keep it open as they didn't want to send their kids to schools further away. I would like to think the morale has increased again. The wisdom shown by the kids who were just getting on with it, is a lesson for us all. Nothing is a done deal until it's signed off, so don't just assume the worst as it may never happen. Make the best you can of every moment and tackle each bridge as you come to it. It has become my mantra. We should listen to the kids more at times.

St Columbas College Catholic Mixed Comprehensive

After Dundonald High School I spent a couple of weeks at St. Columbus College in Strangford. It was a beautiful drive each morning out of Belfast and along the Newtownards peninsula. Getting stuck behind tractors from time to time could be irritating, but the views of the loch were stunning. St. Columbus was a Catholic school. They were extremely welcoming and friendly to me. I enjoyed my couple of weeks there. I had never taught in a Catholic School in Northern Ireland before. There were prayer beads and hail Mary's in assembly and at break, and I was clueless about what was going on. It didn't matter. I was their guest, and I was there to help them out. I taught business studies for a couple of weeks until the teacher off sick came back, and for the limited time I was there I did a good job for them. I have clear memories of St. Columbus and it made me think there should be teacher exchanges between schools, so that more teachers can experience other schools. It could only help to better further the understanding of each other. It would help to educate and open the eyes of everyone to different ways of doing things. I may not have been long at St. Columbus College, but I am very grateful that I had the opportunity to spend some time working there.

Ballyclare Mixed Grammar

My short-term travels continued, and I next spent a couple of months at Ballyclare Grammar school. This was a well-run country grammar school. It was not very far from Belfast, yet it felt like it was in the middle of the country. Like Wallace, Ballyclare had a snooker table in the staffroom. The staff were friendly, the pupils were friendly, and I spent a good couple of months. The thing with short term supply though is that you never really get into the school community, you always remain slightly on the outside as a guest. You don't get involved in running extra-curricular clubs and you don't really get to know the staff well enough to start socialising with them. It was a very interesting few months seeing a few different schools, but short-term supply teaching is not something I would want to do for any long amount of time. It helped me lift myself back up after the shock of leaving Wallace, and it helped me regain my confidence. It also gave me more experience having seen more schools, but after Ballyclare I was ready for longer term placements. I was next to embark on four one-year contracts, followed by a two-year contract. It would be a long path back to the security of being a long term permanent full-time member of staff. It would be a path however that would keep me fresh as I was constantly having to reinvent myself, teach new subjects, and prove myself anew to every school. I didn't have the luxury to get jaded and staid. In many ways I consider myself fortunate, more through luck than judgement I've managed to stay fresh and not bored and cynical like I may have become if I had spent twenty or thirty plus years in the same school.

Hydepark Brethren Mixed Comprehensive

I secured myself a job teaching economics, business studies, and accountancy at Hydepark Brethren School. This was to be yet another eye opener. I didn't know schools like this existed. I had to set up the department from scratch in this school.

The brethren are a closed community and they do not in general let outsiders in. They had to let a few outside teachers in though and I was one of these very few. From my perspective, the brethren community is completely sexist and stuck in the era of The Mayflower circa 1620. Girls do all the domestic chores, marriages are arranged, and there is a pecking order amongst the brethren families. In school any female member of staff who arrived wearing a skirt above the knees was sent home to get changed due to inappropriate attire. The girls always tidied up after the boys despite me telling the boys to tidy up after themselves. The brethren leaders did not like the internet or any newspapers, and if a teacher wanted to show any kind of video it had to be sent off weeks in advance to be edited in Coventry, which I believe is where the head of the brethren in the UK is based. This of course meant I never showed any videos. I was there to run through business studies and accountancy A-levels and get the pupils ready for exams. There was no need for anything else. No extra-curricular, no exposure to the outside world. The science teacher was not allowed to teach the theory of evolution; it was banned by the brethren. Either the sections in the book were ripped out or super glued together. It's hard to believe that a school like this still exists in the UK in the 21st century, but it does.

For all their preaching's on Christianity, the brethren were hypocrites. They paid poorly, and begrudged handing over a pay cheque at the end of each month, and when I say a pay cheque, I literally mean one. They would write a cheque and go to hand it over physically to me, and then almost try to pull it back. It was passive aggressive, and I did not appreciate it. They were distrustful of outsiders and did not treat them in the way you would wish to be treated. In class it was obvious that one of the boys was the son of the richest and most influential family. He therefore believed himself to be in charge and would try and undermine my position as the teacher, sniggering and sniping, yet still needing my help to understand the course content. I had to put him in his place several times, as if you lose control of your classroom then you can no longer perform and teach effectively. No doubt he didn't like it and complained to whoever would listen. I only stayed a year. The school was moving premises further away from Belfast which was a bit far for a daily commute, and I didn't want to spend the rest of my life working for such uncharitable people. I felt sorry for the girls stuck in this life of sexism, but it was not for me to try and change the brethren, that was not my business. However, I couldn't accept their social attitudes as it offended my liberal democratic principles.

Whilst I was there, I did witness one disturbing incident. The school was only a very small building with 30-40 students, it was a few rooms either side of one short corridor. One lesson the pupils had been told to move rooms and arrived at the science teacher's lab. He went berserk and had one of the girls pinned up against the wall, shouting at her and maybe about to hit her. He had lost his job in a previous school due to mental ill-health and should not have been allowed back in the classroom. He only had a couple of years left until retirement, but he had cracked up and lost it. Teaching is a stressful profession, but there is no excuse for this type of behaviour. I saw this from my classroom, and immediately intervened. He dropped the girl who ran off, grateful for my intervention. He then started shouting at me as I tried to calm him down. The vice-principal quickly arrived, and he started shouting at her. The principal of the school then arrived, at whom he also then started shouting at. He was quickly marched off campus and I never saw him again. I have no idea what his final sanction was, but he needed to stop teaching immediately and not set foot in a classroom again, for everyone's sake. These scenes are never pleasant. It shows the importance of mental health, and for schools to recruit appropriate staff. It shows that staff also need mental health support at times, not just the pupils. Fortunately, this type of incident is very rare, but with better support, and better recruitment it can be made even rarer. This helps to explain why teachers must pass a teaching qualification before being allowed to teach. It prevents inappropriate people from ever being allowed to teach in schools, as they are failed during their teacher training. It is why I have never understood how private schools are allowed to hire unqualified teachers. I saw in my later career inappropriate unqualified teachers in private schools who would never have passed their PGCE teaching qualification. They would have been filtered out of the profession. Some of these unqualified teachers wouldn't have lasted even 5 minutes in some of the state schools I have seen.

Newtownbreda High School Mixed Comprehensive

After Hydepark I secured a 1-year maternity cover at Newtownbreda High School. Apparently, the teacher had cracked up and run off to Purdysburn, the mental hospital in Belfast. She had left a mess, and no one knew what to do. The pupils had exam courses to complete, and the management realised they needed an experienced teacher to help. It was again a case of being in the right place at the right time. This time around I also had to teach office and communication systems, ICT, and GCSE maths, in addition to my core subject. Office and communication systems is not an academic subject. It's a list of common-sense definitions linked to working in an office, with things like how to sit at a chair correctly so you don't hurt your back. It's not anything that requires any specific subject knowledge. GCSE maths however does. I hadn't used some of the basic maths myself since leaving school, such as topics like reflections and rotations. It just required a little bit of brushing up and refreshing my memory on some basic maths and definitions and then I was fine. Things like what is a rhombus and what is a parallelogram. To be honest, I've forgotten the difference again since relearning and teaching them. All the resources were provided by the math's department, and I just had to deliver the content. As I wasn't a subject specialist, I was given the bottom set, which seemed fair enough. I inherited a fifth form bottom maths set and I was shocked. After 11 years of schooling, some of them struggled with basic arithmetic and could hardly count. They had given up, and some messed about to hide their inability in maths. I knew some kids didn't like maths, but I didn't expect such a low level. It's a sad fact that some students leave school with such a low level of maths and english. I started to get the trust of the pupils and started to encourage them to work. After a while a few of them started to try again, whilst others started to be pleasant. I felt I was making some difference. After about half a term the head of maths told me in the office that due to getting some of the kids working again, those kids were being moved up a set. I was going to get a few others moving down to the bottom set to replace them. This was a success, but it felt like the reward for my hard work was a punishment. I was to lose the kids I had motivated and get a new bunch to motivate. I just took it in my stride. The thing about moving around schools, is that you soon learn to reinvent yourself, and it becomes easier and easier the more you do it. I was becoming a chameleon. A phoenix rising each time anew in every new school I worked in.

I was in an ICT classroom one day when for some reason the conversation turned around to the police. I suggested the police were there to help and protect us all, and there were a few seconds of silence before one of the boys offered an alternative view. 'No sir, they are just there to prevent us from doing our stuff.' I was teaching boys from the local estate, who did not see a future pathway via studying and university. They were following a different path. They were sons of protestant paramilitaries and were already involved in minor activities of the paramilitary organisation. They accepted me and were opening up and communicating with me. It gave me a glimpse into another world. This is how they saw themselves making a living in the future, and the police just threatened their ability to make money. I have never been sure if I'm working class or middle class, I'm probably somewhere in between the two. I never try to label people, and just try to take everyone as an individual and to judge them on their own merits and behaviour. This alternative view of the police however did surprise my liberal values and did if nothing else add to my worldly understanding of how some others viewed things. I didn't agree with their viewpoint, but I was gaining more invaluable experience with every school I taught in.

Another time in the same class when the pupils asked how I was, I suggested someone was annoying me, and they sat up straight and asked me if I wanted them to sort this person out. I realised what they meant and quickly backtracked saying no thanks, and that all was ok. As an Englishman I was still learning about how things worked in Belfast. They saw me as a Brit, which is why they accepted me. I'm glad the pupils saw me as being on their side, as I don't think if I had been an Irish Republican, they would have accepted me. Not that it should make any difference, but that's Northern Ireland for you.

One afternoon I was covering a class for an absent colleague and had the pupils lined up outside in the corridor waiting to come in when a fight broke out between two of the girls. They were screaming at each other and grabbing at each other. My training would tell me not to get involved but my instincts told me otherwise. I wasn't going to stand there and let two kids hurt each other. I tried to intervene by telling them to stop, which they both ignored, and then I tried to pull them apart. It all happened so quickly. One of the girls started screaming even more, and I realised the other girl was clutching her hair, which as I pulled them apart was causing the girl whose hair was being pulled to scream out in pain. Fortunately, the other girl then let go. I don't know what I would have done otherwise. I ushered the rest of the class in, sent for the head of year, and had to write up an incident report. Nothing was said about me intervening between the two girls to break up a fight. I was a bit worried after everything had cooled down, as these days you aren't allowed to touch students unless to protect them from harm. Common sense said I'd acted in good faith, but you never know. As it was, it all turned out fine, but you only need one unfair allegation in teaching and that can be the end of you. It's why we never close the door when in a one-on-one meeting with a student, it's for our own protection.

Many of the poorly behaved students at Newtownbreda didn't care about detentions. It was the only school I ever worked in that had a dedicated room for the removal of students from class. The small room had 8 individual booths, all facing the wall, where disruptive students would be sent to get on with their work for the day. A teacher was always timetabled to supervise the room, and there was a strict rule of silence. The kids hated it, as they were cut off from their friends and their audience. The removal unit was effective in deterring bad behaviour in class and worked as a discipline policy. It allowed the kids who wanted to learn in class to have a better chance, as it reduced disruptive behaviour. There was a sense of justice to this system, although some people would criticise it for being too Victorian in its approach. All I can say is that it worked, and there are some schools where pupil behaviour has got out of control, and where the introduction of such a system would benefit the learning environment for those who want to learn. It's sad that Newtownbreda felt the need for such a place, but disruptive behaviour is a sad reality of too many schools.

Whilst at Newtownbreda I also became an A-level business studies examiner for the AQA examining board. I got to go to a nice training meeting in a hotel in Manchester and then I was mainly on my own marking scripts that had been posted to me after the exam. Being an examiner is the most boring job I have ever done in education. You get to sit up late after a day's work in school and mark hundreds of scripts. It takes hours and hours and there is a tight deadline. Your scripts are checked by chief examiners to make sure you are not a rogue marker and at the end of the process you eventually earn a few hundred pounds. Being an examiner however does make you a better classroom teacher. It helps you to understand what examiners are looking for, which then helps you teach and coach your students for the exam. In this sense I have no regrets about having become an examiner. The following year the system changed. Scripts were no longer physically posted out to examiners, instead they were scanned electronically by the exam board. Examiners were sent electronic copies of student responses, and you often marked part of questions only. All the part a)'s for example. You were seeded with other examiners and every so often you were stopped as a check to ensure everyone was marking within the tolerance bands set by the chief examiner. Once the seeding checks were completed you could carry on marking, provided you were marking accurately. My problem was that I was marking late at night as I was working during the day, and I was busy with a young family in the evening. Other examiners it seemed were marking during the day as they were probably retired. This meant that when I was stopped to check my marking against other examiners, they weren't marking at night, so I had to wait until the following day to get the go ahead to continue marking. I always got the green light to continue but it wrecked my allocated time slots for marking. I couldn't keep up with the deadline and had to return some scripts. This put me off examining. I had learnt what there was to learn, I didn't really enjoy it, and it didn't pay that well either. After a couple of years, I stopped working as an examiner until I put myself forward again as an IB economics examiner in my last year at ACS. I then only did that for a year as I remembered again how much I disliked marking and being an examiner.

Although I was on long term supply, I was still paid like a daily substitute teacher at Newtownbreda. This means you get no holiday or sick pay, and no occupational pension. The daily rates may look good but when you factor in the lack of the above then you realise it is not quite as attractive financially as it seems at first glance. Supply teachers often don't get paid from the end of June until the end of September and need to survive each year for three months each summer with no pay. It's not an easy gig long term. After the Easter holidays at Newtownbreda I was in the staffroom when another teacher commented that I looked very pale. I rolled up my sleeve and showed them a tube in my arm. Over the Easter holidays I had caught a bacterial infection which had made my face swell up. My doctor sent me home, my wife thankfully sent me back to the doctor who then on second thoughts sent me to A&E. In the hospital they were extremely worried thinking at first that I might have something called Lupus. They then pumped me full of drugs and said they had just caught the infection in time before it had entered my bloodstream and potentially killed me from sepsis. I would be ok, but I would need a nurse to come to my house for a while each evening to pump me full of drugs through a tube in my arm. If I had been a permanent member of staff, I would have taken time off work as I felt terrible and washed out. As a supply teacher I went back to work during the day, whilst the nurse pumped me full of drugs in the evening. I was too poor to be sick and off work. Supply teachers are not as comfortably off as many people believe. There's no sick pay nor holiday pay, and your pension is nothing like that of a full-time permanent member of the teaching staff.

The headmaster of Newtownbreda was both stern with the students, yet also fair and friendly. I really liked him. One time when I was talking to him in his office, he got up and asked me to try out the big chair. Sit in the headmaster's seat. He asked me how it felt and if I liked it. I must say that just for a moment it felt good. However, I have never aspired to climb up into management. I entered teaching to stay in the classroom and to teach the kids. This is what inspires me and drives me, not to be involved in endless meetings and bureaucracy. It's the daily contact with the pupils that is the magic of teaching. It's about the rapport you build with young people who have their entire life still in front of them. It's their energy and enthusiasm that keeps you going, and which keeps you young. Lose that and you lose yourself as a teacher. It is about caring and wanting to make a difference and helping youngsters to succeed. To be the headmaster or headmistress of a school is a completely different job, and not one I would want. The head is a lonely figure. Often the staff moan about the head, as they don't like all the decisions that are being imposed on them from above. At times I have felt like this as well. Heads do not have an easy job. They have a budget that is often lacking, yet they have all these demands placed upon them to improve their school. Parents are often complaining to them. They are required to deal with external agencies at times like the police or maybe even the media. They need to lead and direct their staff and control discipline within the school. It is a thankless task, yet also a vital one. A good headmaster or headmistress is the making of a school, a bad one is the opposite, the breaking of a school. I have seen different types of heads in schools. There is the bureaucratic head who writes policies and who stays in their office all the time. They implement procedures on staff, and often drive through changes in a school that are required by OFSTED inspectors. They are appointed to write policies and are effective in the short-term when policies need to be drawn up. The worst type of head is the dictatorial type. The autocrat who doesn't communicate and listen to staff. The type who is mediocre at best and yet due to their own inflated ego believe themselves to be something special. This type of head can be very destructive, often leading to a fall in staff morale and a turnover of teaching staff who refuse to work under such conditions. They might achieve a goal of cutting costs as older more experienced staff leave to be replaced by younger more pliable teachers who will do what the bullying head demands, but they do so at the expense of the sense of community that has been built up over the years amongst staff. This type of head needs to be sacked and removed as a matter of urgency however, as in the long run they harm a school. I only ever encountered this type of headmaster once, in the later days of my time at ACS International. I'm glad to say he didn't last too long at ACS. The best type of head is one who inspires the entire community. They are visible and often to be seen in the corridors. They know everyone by name, the staff, the pupils, the parents, everyone. They live and breathe the school. They are both fair yet stern. Such a head will back up staff if attacked unfairly by parents, but who will also roast staff for doing something they shouldn't and will demand better in the future. This type of head demands respect, and you will give them extra and follow them. They are not just managers, they are leaders. I felt this way about the headmaster at Newtownbreda.

Mind you that didn't stop me from protecting myself at his expense at the annual school formal. It was a weekend and one of the boys arrived already off his face and went straight to the toilets. How he got in I don't know, but I think his friends must have got him past the front door. The teachers quickly noticed, and the headmaster was straight on to it. He confronted the boy and phoned his parents to come and collect him immediately. He would be in trouble on Monday when school was open again. The headmaster asked me to help walk the boy out to his parents. The boy was so drunk he could barely stagger. I took one arm, and the headmaster another. As we were walking the boy's head tilted to my shoulder and I started to hear a churning sound. No way was he going to vomit all over me! I lifted my shoulder instantly and his head flopped over and tilted towards the headmaster instead. Just in time for him to vomit all over the unsuspecting headmaster. I may have liked the headmaster, but I didn't like him enough to be peuked all over. The boy was now really going to be in big trouble come Monday morning. He shouldn't have arrived at the formal completely off his head with drink. He had pre-loaded with alcohol as by then drink was no longer allowed to be served at formals. Call it the law of unintended consequences if you will.

Royal School Dungannon Mixed Grammar

Again, the year contract came to an end, and I was once again cast adrift. I'd had a good year at Newtownbreda. The fact that it was only a 10 minutes' drive from my house was also a boon, as it helped me to get home earlier and relieve Hilda my mother-in-law from looking after our 2 young sons. Childcare is so expensive, without the help of my wife's mum when the kids were young, I don't know how we would have financially coped.

Now however I would have to drive 45 minutes down the motorway to Dungannon towards the west of Northern Ireland. I had secured another 1-year maternity contract at a good grammar school called the Royal School Dungannon. This time along with more ICT I had to teach geography and LLW employability in addition to both A-level economics and A-level business studies, plus GCSE business studies.

I enjoyed the drive to Dungannon in my car. Every morning I'd put on radio 2 and listen to Chris Evans. He's always been my favourite radio star. It's a great way to wake up listening to the radio. I should listen more when I'm at home, but like many people I tend to listen more in my car when travelling to and from work.

Royal School Dungannon or RSD for short was one of my favourite schools of all time I have ever taught in. It was a nice quiet country mixed grammar school. The pupils and staff were all both very friendly and respectful. The headmaster was a decent and fair individual, which is what you hope for in a head. This was perhaps the first time where I was starting to feel a little bit older and no longer one of the younger staff. Maybe I had been starting to feel like this at Newtownbreda, it's something that creeps up on you. I was in the staffroom for example, and we were talking about football, one of the most common topics of all amongst men. For some reason FA cup finals came up, and someone was listing Manchester United FA cup finals. Lots of people in Northern Ireland support either Manchester United or Liverpool, and as a Tottenham fan I had grown used to this. The younger member of staff was then saying Manchester United were in the 1979 FA cup final and was trying to recollect the score. I told him it was 3-2 to Arsenal with Liam Brady crossing to the far post to Alan Sunderland who scored the winner past Gary Bailey the Man Utd goalkeeper. He looked at me with doubt in his eyes, so I told him I remember because I watched it live at the time. I was 10, and back then the FA cup final was huge being the biggest sporting event of the entire year. I told him I clearly remembered. With doubt he picked up his phone and googled the 1979 FA cup final, before confirming I was right because the internet said so. I looked at the other older guy with a knowing shake of my head. What were these youngsters like? Little did I know that this was just the start of things to come. iPads and iPhones have changed life in so many ways. Younger generations are now addicted to their devices and tap for immediate answers all the time. They no longer seem to need to hold information for themselves and doubt the word of a real live person who was there over the second-hand information on the internet. I am a people person, so the thought of listening to machines over people is something I find abhorrent. I think this little episode was the first time it really sank in for me just how much these devices and the internet were taking over. I was the last generation pre-internet, whilst not being that old when the internet and mobiles came along. However, I would never embrace mobiles and iPads quite like the youngsters who were growing up with them. Over the next 10 years this would only become even more true as kids were now being born into a world already with these devices and knew nothing else. I had grown up playing football in the streets and riding about on my bike. I'd grown up in the real world not a virtual one, and I was starting to see the world rapidly changing away from what I had known. My own kids were iPad kids, it was becoming a brave new world that I was only just about able to understand.

At the end of the Christmas term the school went over to the local church for the end of term service. This was quite normal, but what awaited me in my experience certainly was not. As the service got going a Presbyterian minister started giving his sermon. The only thing was that he was dressed in a Hawaiian shirt, which I thought was a bit bizarre. He then started launching into how God loves us all but that we are all sinners and that we shall all suffer eternal damnation. Now I don't know about you, but I certainly don't want to burn in hell. He was putting the fear of God into all the schoolchildren. As an Englishman, who's not overly religious, I rejected fully his preaching and found the whole show horrific. Parents had sent their kids to school in the morning for an education, they had not chosen to send them to church and be subjected to such fear induced brainwashing. Schools and churches need to be kept separate. If someone wants to go to church outside of school hours then fine, but religion should be kept out of schools as much as possible. This eternal damnation rant was shocking, and yet no one else seemed in the slightest bit perturbed. At the end of the blistering sermon, we all piled back over to the school and the end of the Christmas term. In the staffroom I raised my unease over what had just happened with some other teachers, who just shrugged saying it was Northern Ireland and they didn't put anything by it. I was an Englishman and didn't understand Presbyterians, but I'd get used to such things. No, I won't. Vicars as I call them in Hawaiian shirts spouting fire and brimstone should not be allowed anywhere near schools. It is one of the few times I have been offended during my career, and this hell and damnation speech had truly offended me on several levels. I took a deep breath, calmed down, and moved on. I'd be damned if I was going to hell, I was going home instead to stuff myself with turkey and over-indulge in wine. I intended to enjoy myself fully over the festive period.

It's whilst I was at Dungannon that I had my first run in with the inspectors. The vice principal told me that an inspector was in to look at school policies and procedures, but as an ex-business studies teacher was interested in sitting in on one of my lessons. He would not be there to officially inspect my teaching so there was no pressure, it was just a curiosity on behalf of the inspector and welcoming on behalf of the school. What else could I do but agree to the request. I do not like inspectors. I often do not agree with their subjective views on education and the fact that they parachute in during the middle of a two-year course when you are trying to get through a syllabus and prepare the students for the final exams. Often you can get around this with a bit of forewarning, and deliver a lesson geared for the inspectors. A lesson where you have already previously taught the class the topic, and in which you then spend the lesson being observed on a follow up activity. A good example is cash-flow forecasting, you teach the content the lesson before and let the inspector observe the class constructing and filling out cash-flows on the computer. This is not however what happened at RSD as I hadn't any warning about the inspector, so I had to go with the lesson I had planned, which was a theory lesson. It is essential to teach theory, without teaching some theory the students will fail exams, and they are not capable of always teaching themselves theory. At the end of the lesson, the inspector who was a guest and who was not there to judge me asked me what I called what he had observed. I replied that I called it teaching, to which his riposte was, that is where you went wrong you should be a facilitator. This was the first time I ever heard this phrase, and it was a phrase that seemed to grow over the next decade. I was outraged, this old out of touch inspector parachutes in with no understanding of the pressures of teaching to an external exam and criticises the teacher for teaching! Parents want their kids to get good grades, so do management, and so do the kids themselves. If you followed the instructions of the inspectors, then the kid's grades would fall. It's madness. Let the teachers teach, it's what we do best. We the teachers are the professionals. Knowing that this inspector had no authority and was just a guest, I quickly told him to facilitate his way out of my classroom and not to come back. The vice principal Richard later came scurrying down to ask what I had done to his inspector. After a brief chat he told me to carry on with my teaching, and to let him deal with the inspector. That was fine by me.

Dungannon had a small boarding wing, and although there were dedicated boarding staff, all the regular teaching staff were also expected to work one night a term on the boarding rota. I had never been on boarding before, so this was all new to me at the time. It was quite easy, you just had to stay until 10pm and sit around the boarding staff common room drinking cups of tea. The full-time boarding staff had everything under control, and you felt more like their guest for the evening. Of course, in an emergency they would need your help, but I was only ever there on evenings where everything ran smoothly. You also ate dinner with the boarders and got to chat with a few of the pupils. It did help me understand my boarding students back in the classroom the following day though, as you got a better understanding of where they were coming from. There weren't many schools with boarding left in Northern Ireland at that time. Many of the RSD boarders were from Hong Kong, and I asked some of them what made them choose to board in Dungannon in Northern Ireland instead of for example somewhere in England. They all replied that the fees were much cheaper and that their parents thought it was better value for money. I couldn't fault their logic. It is true that compared to the South of England the cost of living is much lower and therefore the quality of life for the average employed person is higher in Northern Ireland. Northern Ireland is a hidden gem, but there was no hiding it from the Hong Kongers who had done their research. Fair play to them, why pay more than necessary.

I've been on many school trips, often just day trips, but whilst I was at RSD, I decided to organise a residential trip over in London. At Wallace I used to go on the annual french trip, but I never organised them. There are companies that you just pay, and they do most of it for you, so organising trips is not too difficult. The main thing is collecting in the money, and once you have enough students the trip is on. As soon as I put a few hours of shopping on the agenda the pupils started to sign up. The Bank of England tour it seemed was just an excuse for a shopping trip to London. On the trip itself you need to make sure you have all the passports and documentation. You need to find coach drivers and make sure everything is ok at the hotel. You are constantly checking to make sure you haven't lost any of the students. There is no way I'd organise something like a ski trip as it's almost guaranteed that someone will end up in hospital with a broken leg or something. It's also easier when you stay in your own country and there is no language barrier. Still, it was another experience and string to my bow to organise a residential trip. The trip itself went smoothly, with me constantly checking to make sure I hadn't lost any of the pupils. My main memories were more of organising the trip than of the trip itself. The small museum at The Bank of England as I recall was mildly interesting, but I've been to London so many times that the rest of it just became a blur.

Towards the end of the year, it was becoming apparent that the government was slashing school budgets. The country was coming out of the banking crisis and was in recession. The headmaster one break time in his weekly briefing told us all that it was getting so bad that if it continued, he would have to shut the school and hang a closed sign up on the school gates. Scones would no longer be freely provided for staff at break time on a Friday, there wasn't the money. This was all quite alarming. The Entitlement Framework had already squeezed me out of a permanent job in Northern Ireland, and this was starting to shape up as something that could hurt supply work. Up until then the local education authorities had paid for substitute teachers out of their budget, but now substitute teachers were going to be paid out of school budgets. Whether you were covering a one-year maternity, or were just working a few days in a school, you were still a substitute teacher. For me this was another blow. I was at the top of the teacher pay salary due to all my experience. Schools liked to employ me as a sub when the local education authority was paying, but I instantly realised would not be willing to hire me if they had to pay for me out of their own budget. It was an ominous sign. Schools were facing an unprecedented squeeze on their budgets, and it was obvious that they would start hiring younger cheaper substitute teachers. Not only had I been squeezed out of permanent work, I would also soon be squeezed out of substitute teaching work. The sub-prime mortgage crisis that started in America was about to explode in my face. I left RSD without work for the following year and told my fears to my wife. I doubted I'd get another job in Northern Ireland. She brushed this off and said all would be fine once September came around.

London Calling

By October half-term we were desperate. I needed a job otherwise we wouldn't be able to pay for the mortgage. I still had a young family to help support. It was decided with my wife that I would have to go and look for work in London, and quickly. I needed a job by the New Year otherwise we would lose the house. The pressure was on.

Fortunately, we had a family friend called Joanna who lived in London and who was happy to put me up cheaply. She rented out rooms in her house to people she knew and without her help I would have either lost my house, or I would have had to work away from home without being able to afford to come back at weekends. I owe her an eternal debt of gratitude. At times we all need some help, and I needed all the help I could get. I'm also very grateful to my father-in-law Ed who drove me back and forth to the airport in Belfast every week whilst I worked away from home in London. We had many interesting chats putting the world to rights during the hours and hours spent together in the car. Ed also told me many interesting stories about absolutely everything and anything. I think he enjoyed both the audience and the drive.

I soon went for an interview in a mixed comprehensive school in Streatham in South London in early November. The school didn't look great, but I was desperate, and I would have taken anything. The headmaster that day did me a huge favour. After the interview he told me I was the most experienced candidate but that I would most likely only stay a year and move on when I found something better. He was right. He needed someone who would stay longer, so with that in mind he offered the job to another candidate. Inwardly I agreed with him, and if he hadn't made this decision my career path would have taken a different turn to what it was about to take. I carried on with my job hunting, and it wasn't long before I found a job more to my liking in London. My luck was holding out. I started in the late November at Bellerbey's College in Greenwich.

Bellerbey's College Mixed International

Bellerbey's was a private college that sourced international students and then taught them foundation courses. It has links with many UK universities that pay Bellerbey's for finding lucrative international students and making sure they are ready for university entrance by teaching foundation courses in english and specialist subjects. I was back to teaching both economics and business studies. Some of the students were even post grads who were following foundation courses to go on and do a masters course in UK universities. Teaching a class of students who are 22, is not the same as teaching a class of students who are 18. Students who are 22-year-olds are more mature and are adults, however they are still just students wanting to learn and you are still the teacher they look up to for guidance and support to help them get through the exam.

Bellerbey's didn't have a school uniform, which after so many years of teaching in schools was a bit strange at first. There are arguments for and against school uniforms. They do allow teachers to often focus discipline on low level uniform infringements, which does help to keep conflicts from escalating. Also, it is argued that with no uniform poorer students who can't afford expensive brands will be made to feel inferior. I personally don't like uniforms as I think they are too formal. I just prefer to talk to students and gain respect through my subject knowledge, organised courses, and friendly and fair demeanour. All whilst expecting students to put in the effort required to succeed. For me it was like a breath of fresh air to be at an educational establishment without school uniforms. Not everyone sees it my way, but I would scrap school uniforms tomorrow if it was my decision. In France for example I witnessed schools that don't have school uniforms, and it doesn't harm their education. School uniforms seems to be a British thing.

The feel of Bellerbey's was completely different to all the other schools I had taught in. There was an open plan office come staff room where everyone had a desk. This was your base, and where you would sit in free lessons. Other schools just have a general staffroom, and all the teachers have a desk in their own classrooms. I hate open plan offices. There's too much noise and a lack of privacy. I was very happy when teaching classes at Bellerbey's, but I didn't like being in the open plan office. It felt like you had no personal space to call your own.

I also enjoyed the international students. I had been an international student myself when I was at university in the town of Rennes in Brittany, France, and I have always been interested in other people and other cultures. International schools are such a rich mix of interesting staff and students, and I found teaching international students extremely interesting. I was always learning new facts and details about new countries. It's amazing how well all the international students get on with each other, if only the rest of the world could do the same. Of course, international students often come from wealthy backgrounds and don't suffer from poverty. They also tend to be well travelled and more open to others, plus they are better educated about other countries and have a global outlook. In some ways international communities are like an extra nationality. They get on better with other international people who travel around, and although are from a certain country, they sometimes no longer fit in back home. This was my first experience of teaching international students, and I felt lucky to have the opportunity. It helped when one boy from South Korea professed that he wanted to be just like me when he grew up. Maybe he wanted higher marks, or maybe I really made a positive impact on him. That's the thing with teaching, you never know who you have impacted in a positive way and who's lives you may have enriched. It explains why teaching is such an important role. It is more than just about imparting knowledge; it's about setting an example and being a positive role model to the next generation.

My commute to Bellerbey's was a killer. I had to get up in North London at 5.15am to get the tube to Bank and change for the Docklands Light Railway or

DLR all the way to Greenwich. It was then a 10 minutes' walk to Bellerbey's. I would then return in the evening, and at weekends commute back to Belfast on a Friday night before returning to London on a Sunday night. I was commuting on average around 24 hours a week. This is a ridiculous amount of time to be commuting each week. I managed to read many books whilst commuting, including some classics like The Grapes of Wrath, Stoner, The Great Gatsby, All Quiet on the Western Front, Heart of Darkness, To Kill a Mockingbird, plus various textbooks on history, economics, and business management. The DLR has no drivers, so it was fun to sit at the front of the train and see the tube tracks and tunnels in front of you. You get to feel like a tube driver. Back in North London every night I would end up talking with Joanna the family friend who was putting me up. She would often get out a bottle of Haut-Médoc red wine which was my favourite and keep me up late talking, sometimes until nearly 2am. As an opera singer, I would often hear Joanna and other opera singer friends of hers who also lodged with her when I got back to the house. I would jokingly pretend they all sounded the same, but in truth I got to quite like hearing them all singing. Joanna gave me a welcoming base and made my transition back to London as good as could be hoped for. It was exhausting however commuting every day across London, and every weekend back to Belfast. It was something that just had to be done, so I rolled up my sleeves and made the best of it.

Every morning in Greenwich I would walk past the Cutty Sark the famous old tea clipper that sailed the oceans during the 1870s. I would often get breakfast in a nearby coffee shop. Sometimes during a lunch break I would stroll down to Greenwich to wander around the market and look at the famous tea clipper. If I had a little longer, I might even walk up to Greenwich Conservatory and beyond to Black Heath. On one of these occasions, I saw the Queen and the Duke of Edinburgh opening the Cutty Sark once more to the public. They were up on the deck in plain sight. It's only the 2nd time I've seen the Queen. I've seen Charles once, as well as William and Harry when they were young on different occasions. Always when I've just been out and about. I have a great deal of admiration for the Queen, which is always appreciated when I'm back home in Belfast amongst the protestant community. Commuting to Greenwich on the DLR, and spending time around the Cutty Sark, and teaching international students was a stroke of good fortune. Seeing as I needed to work away in London, if I had ended up in the tough comprehensive that I had first interviewed for, then I imagine I would have been less happy. I do acknowledge my blessings and my good fortune.

Bellerbey's ran a talent show one night in a nearby venue. I am always amazed by the diverse talents of the students. Some are great musicians, others great singers, and that night on display there was also a great magician. He seemed to have an endless number of cards that just kept on appearing from nowhere. I was mesmerized. However much I teach students in class to succeed in economics and business studies, it is always great to see their other talents. Although not on show that night, I'm sure many of the students were also very talented in the sporting field. Extra-curricular always leads to great discussions in class and help to build the rapport between the teacher and the student. It's showing that you are interested, as well as knowledgeable, that often helps to inspire students to work that extra little bit.

I enjoyed my time at Bellerbey's. I was working with the daughter of the guy who wrote the national textbooks which also added a bit of kudos to the job. However, I had a problem with the summer holiday dates. In Northern Ireland the schools break up for the summer at the end of June, in time for July 12th and the marching season. The school holidays last all the way through to the end of August. Many schools in England don't break up until later in July. This would have ruined my family summer holidays. Bellerbey's worked through the summer, and you could either choose the early holidays which started at the end of June for 4 weeks, or the later holidays that started at the end of July. Either did not fit well with my family. I decided to take the early holidays that started at the end of June, and to leave Bellerbey's. I could only do this because I had secured yet another job, this time at ACS Cobham International School. As it had American roots it also broke up for the summer holidays at the end of June, because they wanted to be on holiday for July 4th. They didn't go back until late August. I had been very lucky once again. There could be hardly any schools in London with similar summer holiday dates to schools in Belfast, plus it was an international school and I realised just how much I liked international students and staff.

The Later Years 2012 – 2022

ACS Mixed International

ACS stands for American Community College. ACS happened by chance. I had realised that Bellerbey's holidays didn't suit me, so I started to look for jobs. At this stage I wasn't ready to fill out application forms as I was just having a quick first glance. I came across an advert that suggested I put in my CV. That was quick and easy to do, and the next thing I heard was to come to the office of Harris Hill recruitment agency, and yes, you've guessed it when I was there, they got me to fill out an application form. As luck would have it, ACS were just looking for an economics and business teacher, as I started looking for a new school. A few years later ACS stopped using recruitment agencies and started appointing staff through international job fairs. I would never have known about such things, so it was very much a case of being in the right place at the right time. Harris Hill drilled me for the interview and sent me down to ACS. I got the job, and it was to become the school I would spend the longest time in.

I loved ACS. I still do. I loved the teachers and the students. I loved the reception and office staff, Will, Clare, and Amanda who always helped and always had time for a smile and a friendly chat. At the time when I arrived it was nothing like any other school I had ever encountered. There were no head of years, that was to come later. There were no head of departments either. What I thought was my HOD, soon told me that he was more my mentor than a head of department. I had a syllabus and I had classes, and it was up to me to deliver my courses how I wanted. I was the boss of my own classroom, with no interference from management. If I didn't deliver the parents would soon complain to the headmaster, who would then pull me up and either tell me off or sack me. This might have been a nightmare for new inexperienced teachers, but for me it was blissful. I had autonomy. This was how teaching should be. The other economics teacher was an older Californian dude called Rob, who was very helpful and just an all-round great guy. He had read so much throughout his life that he had an extensive knowledge of the subject. He was my guru. He is the best economics colleague I have ever known, and when I started at ACS, he took me under his wing and helped me along. My mentor, who I looked at as my HOD was a history teacher called Adam. He also had immense knowledge, and later went on to write an academic book called

Soldiering On, of which I proudly own a signed copy. I was surrounded by older guys who all knew so much. I was in a social sciences faculty, rather than a narrow economics and business department. This helped to see the overlapping areas between the social sciences, which further deepened my own understanding of my main subject economics.

At ACS I was teaching the IB, or International Baccalaureate. I had moved away from teaching A-levels. The IB in my opinion is more rigorous than A-levels. You study 6 subjects, 3 at higher level and 3 at standard level. You must pick a science and a maths course among them, so it offers a wider education than the narrow A-levels. Students on the IB also must complete a 4500-word extended essay which is more like a piece of work you would expect at the first year of university. They then also need to complete some community service called CAS hours, and lastly, they must complete TOK or theory of knowledge, which is a course in different ways of thinking as I understand it. The IB prepares students better for university but is a tough ask. The workload on the students, especially in the senior year is intense. I soon realised that the IB economics course was similar in many ways to the old A-level course I had taught back in the mid to late 1990s. There was some coursework and a final exam at the end of 2 years. There were no modular exams and countless resits, and there were no external exams at the end of the first year of the course, as is the case with AS exams. I quickly realised I preferred teaching the IB to A-levels. Not only did I prefer the way the course was examined, but also many resources were provided free on the internet by other IB teachers. This is unlike A-levels where resources on the internet often require you to pay money. IB teachers it seemed provided resources solely for the added prestige. The school was also very well-funded, so there was no problem with every student having a textbook, and there was no limit on the amount of photocopying I wanted to do. Teachers were even provided with an Apple Mac computer and an iPad. It was almost all sounding too good to be true.

I was also given the opportunity to teach world history. I love history, along with my own subject economics. After all these years and all the courses that I had been asked to teach, I was finally being asked to teach history. ACS was organised along American lines, and I was working in the high school. I was teaching history to what would be the GCSE age groups in a British school. The only thing was that they were not studying for an external exam at the end of the course, it was just an internal exam. I couldn't understand this for a few weeks and then I discovered something called GPA, or grade point average.

The course wasn't geared up for an end of 2-year external exam, but rather on rolling internal grades throughout the course. Each grade went into the gradebook and grades were then averaged out. Higher grades pulled your average up, and lower grades pulled your average down. We had a gradebook that parents could see 24/7, so everyone always knew how they were doing. Both parents and the students were obsessed with GPA. As parents paid extremely high fees you had to keep the customers happy to keep the management happy. GPA even crept into my IB courses. The IB is set up as a 2-year course with an end of course exam. For students wishing to go to UK universities this was fine, however there were students on the IB who were planning on going to American universities. American universities are more interested in GPA. This was a problem, as I wasn't teaching a GPA course in IB economics, I was preparing students for an end of 2-year exam. I was not looking to do lots of weekly short quizzes for GPA, but rather bring the students up to speed on writing essays and constructing technical diagrams. You have no choice but to prioritise, so my solution was to nod to GPA by setting tasks that didn't ruin the average scores, whilst targeting primarily getting ready for the end of year exams. It seemed to work.

I remember in one of my early classes discussing macroeconomics, and government responses to issues such as inflation, unemployment, and interest rates. One of my students raised his hands and suggested I was wrong. I quoted my source as the Financial Times and asked what his was. He replied that his dad was on the politburo in China and that the official figures were incorrect. What could I say to that! What's more, one of the Russian boys, who was the son of an oligarch was quickly taking notes. State economic secrets were passing across in my lesson. Welcome again to ACS. With a shake of my head, I quickly moved on with my lesson.

The students were all extremely polite, although they didn't divulge much about their lives outside of school. Some of the teachers who had been at the school for years told me there used to be a helipad, and that some of the kids in the past had security guards to protect them from being kidnapped. The school not only held fire drills, but also held lockdown drills should a gunman ever enter the campus. We would all huddle in silence behind the locked classroom door away from sight until the password 'cupcakes' was announced across the internal Tanoy system. One time in my later years at ACS there was a hoax bomb scare which was taken very seriously. It was after school, and the entire dorm was evacuated to the canteen area whilst police swarmed the campus with sniffer dogs and drones. The police even despatched a helicopter which hovered overhead. No expense was spared to make sure the wealthy kids were protected. Another member of staff asked me if I was worried with the helicopter hovering overhead, I just laughed and said it reminded me of back home in Belfast, where helicopters used to hover over the city constantly. I think my colleague was a bit stunned, as the comfort of Surrey was a million miles away from the lived reality of the legacy of The Troubles in Belfast.

This was a completely different world. Upper sixth were called seniors, lower sixth were called juniors, and invigilating exams was called proctoring. Staff and students came from all corners of the world. You would learn something new every day. ACS was a bubble of comfort and wealth, and the sunny uplands that many wish to aspire to. Or at least so it appears on the surface. Wealthy individuals are people too with problems. Some students had been dumped on the dorm by their parents, whilst their parents traversed around the world. Students had high expectations placed upon them often by their parents, although for many if they failed, they would still be fine. They could enter the family business, or just be kept by their rich parents. Still money didn't create happiness, although there was no denying that a certain amount helped. All the students had Apple Macs, iPads and iPhones, and expensive clothes. Some only travelled on private jets, for them first class was roughing it. They were still just my students and were all in my class to learn. I enjoyed teaching them all. I have to say they were always very nice to me. One of my all-time favourite students was called Suleman. He always had a smile and was always ready to help me out with any technical issues with my computer. He would have gone on to do great things in this world, I am sure. Tragically a year after leaving ACS he took a trip on the ill-fated Titanic sub with his father and a few others, and never came back. I loved Suleman and shall always remember his smiling face in both my IB economics and IB business management classes. May his soul rest in peace.

One break time all the teachers of one student called Boris were called down to the administration room for a meeting with the headmaster and the boy's parent. The parent was a Russian oligarch and had been named by the CIA as the Merchant of Death for selling weapons during the 1990s after the collapse of the Soviet Union. The boy pointed at me and one other teacher, my heart stopped, and then he said, "Those two are ok." I breathed again. The headmaster then dismissed the pair of us and roasted all the other teachers. I was just glad not to be in the bad books of the Merchant of Death. I have never left a room so quickly.

ACS, like many of these private schools, is really benefiting from blood money. The fees being paid could often have come from dodgy sources, but they had been washed through the UK banks first and declared clean. As far as the school was concerned that meant the money was ok. It was a dirty business model, but that is the reality of power and wealth when you start to see it up closer. ACS may be called a school, but I soon realised that it is ruled by money and is in fact really a business in the field of education. Business choices would always trump educational choices. You could ignore this in your day-to-day teaching by spending your time with the faculty and the students, but once you started talking to management, admissions, finance, and marketing, you realised you worked for a business primarily and not a school. HR were often on the side of the money rather than the staff.

Money was everywhere. One student had a problem of running out of money every month. He was 17 and getting into night clubs by bribing the doormen. He would then spend the rest of the night showing off and buying £800 bottles of champagne. It turned out that his monthly budget of £15000 was not enough. When this was realised, the solution was simple, just raise his monthly allowance to £17000. Lack of money was never an issue.

Another student couldn't be bothered to walk 5 steps to pick up the £50 note he had dropped, and when I picked it up and walked over and put it in his hand, he then could hardly be bothered to put it in his pocket. They had too much money and didn't comprehend how £20 is a lot of money to a lot of people. I never have £50 notes in my wallet and hadn't been brought up with excess money. I had been lucky to grow up in a comfortable enough background, but I still found their lack of respect for money as both slightly disturbing and offensive.

But everyone was still always so nice and pleasant, I guess they could afford to be.

Taxi drivers that took me to the airport each week would sometimes tell me that some of the kids did drugs, some of the wives were unhappy trophy wives whilst their rich husbands were away having affairs. The rich have their problems; they are just different ones to the rest of us.

My commute each evening back up to North London from ACS was made easier by making a best friend who also travelled on the ACS bus, and who took the train back up to Waterloo. After a few months of chatting, and sharing a few drinks in some pubs, he revealed that he was the Prince of Montenegro, and a relative of the Romanov family that were deposed during the Russian Revolution. Many European royal families were deposed and either killed or fled during the early twentieth century, his had been one of them who had fled to Britain. To me he was just my mate Milan, a maths and physics teacher who worked at ACS with me. I was just a village boy, and I was now rubbing shoulders with royalty, albeit deposed, penniless, and not the first in line. I spent many nights out with him, one at the liberal club in central London, another as a VIP guest at a restaurant with a Harley Street Doctor, and others just as a regular punter at the Vinoteque bar in Surbiton where the welcoming Romanian owner gave us free drinks from time to time. When you commute and work away from home, friendly faces just make it easier to make it through.

Other friends on the staff bus were Sam, Michael, and Svetlana. They all helped ease my commute and being away from home each week with their friendly chat. Sam who was from the USA always told such great stories, Michael was a friendly Australian chancer, and Svetlana was my Ukrainian friend who'd not had it easy to say the very least. I always felt that I wanted to help her if I could, she deserved a break.

The idea when I went to London was not to stay there for too long, however finding teaching jobs in Northern Ireland is extremely difficult. I was beginning to get older, was more expensive, and was no longer teaching A-levels but the IB instead. It was getting harder and harder to get a teaching job back in Belfast. I couldn't afford not to work so I was in a catch 22 situation. I had to work away from home, but I really wanted to be at home with my family. I was juggling two different lives. I would go home every weekend and holiday and be away during the week. I had signed a two-year contract at ACS, and at the end of it after discussions with my wife, I decided to leave and get a job as a HOD teaching A-levels in an all-boys private school in Surrey on the outskirts of London. I didn't want to leave ACS, but the thought was by teaching A-levels again and being a HOD it might help me get back to Belfast. Not really much chance of that but I decided to try. I left ACS with a heavy heart after two great years and went to Ewell Castle. It wouldn't be long before I was back at ACS.

Ewell Castle All Boys Private

Ewell Castle is at the lower end of British private schools, and as an all-boys school it had some poorly behaved students. I had a nice office and was HOD, but I never truly liked my time at Ewell Castle. I think I never really wanted to leave ACS, and I missed all my friends and all the international students. The other teacher in my department was unfriendly and sneaky. He was annoyed as he had wanted to be the HOD, and he obstructed everything to try and make me fail. If I had decided to stay longer, I would have had to sort him out and put him in his place as a matter of urgency.

Alongside A-level economics, and A-level business studies, I was also teaching A-level politics. This was enjoyable, as my degree had British politics in it, and I'd studied economics for a better understanding of how to fund policies that increased equality and living standards for all. Economics, politics, and history were my academic passions. The economics course was split between 3 different teachers. This was a nightmare and ludicrous. It made it so much harder to organise and deliver the course. I immediately knew this was a problem and something that I fundamentally disagreed with. Unfortunately, the headmaster fundamentally believed in it, and there was no meeting of minds. I knew I would not stay long, as this was a real issue for me. One of the co-teachers was a maths teacher and needed my help with the content, and as it turned out he was better than the business studies teacher in my department who didn't know any economics either. I have found that business studies teachers struggle to teach economics as they often lack the linear thinking skills. Give me a maths teacher any day over a business studies teacher to train up in economics. All this just added to the already high workload. The GCSE business studies class was full of badly misbehaved boys, and it reminded me of my early days back at Northwood Hills Comprehensive. I did not enjoy these classes. I was beginning to think I should have stayed at ACS where I had been happy.

After a couple of months, I received an email from one of my former lower sixth students at ACS called Gabriella, who was now in her senior year. She was asking for me to write her a reference for university, and the ACS counsellors had given her my email. I was fine with that and just asked how things were. I was not expecting the reply I received. She told me the teacher who had replaced me was awful, and could I please come back. Apparently, all the parents were unhappy and were threatening to sue the school. I emailed my mentor Adam, or as I considered him my HOD at ACS and asked him what was going on. After a few exchanges he asked me if I would come back, all unofficial but with the knowledge of the ACS management. I spoke to my wife and told her I thought this was a good idea, and then I contacted my old HOD Adam and said I was prepared to come back, but I had to get out of my contract at Ewell Castle. The ACS students started to hear rumours and the ball started rolling. I started to let my GCSE business studies class get out of control, and soon got complaints. I told the headmaster at Ewell Castle I wanted to go back to ACS, and that they wanted me. I also luckily was put on cover and found on a desk, notes from an unofficial classroom inspection, which were making official complaints about my GCSE class. I took photos of this on my mobile phone as evidence. I held this against them as well. The headmaster in a meeting told me I was a sixth form teacher, and that I had 48 hours to do a deal with ACS. I went the next day back to ACS, negotiated a pay rise to match my HOD salary at Ewell Castle, and started working again at ACS at the start of January. I only spent one term in the end at Ewell Castle. I did however learn that I didn't overly like teaching in an all-boys school, and that the staff you work with are vital. At ACS everyone I worked with in the social studies department was my friend and I trusted them all. At Ewell Castle the other member of my department had been undermining, dishonest, and not to be trusted. I was happy to leave Ewell Castle and go back to ACS. I was lucky that the teacher who had replaced me had been so bad, otherwise I would never have had the chance for a second homecoming. Such is life. The next 7 years would be the best in my entire teaching career. ACS may not have helped me to get back home to Belfast, but at least it made me happy when I was away during the week and paid me relatively well.

ACS Mixed International Continued

My second homecoming was greeted with cheers from my students when I walked back into the classroom. They were of the mind that their IBs and their futures had just been saved. It was very emotional. In the end that class did very well in their IB exams, I think the motivational lift of my return helped them surge past the finish line.

I was now teaching both IB economics and IB business management, and instead of world history I had been tasked with teaching global studies. This for me was a delight. It was a class where you decided what topics to teach and how to assess them. There was no exam, just course credits. I would run through ethical and moral topics, interspersed with geopolitical topics, I'd usually show a short video, follow it up with a classroom discussion and then set a written homework. It seemed to work well, and the students enjoyed it. For IB economics I had discovered resources on the internet. I uploaded digital notes onto my first ever digital platform called Edmodo, and I ran educational videos in class. I would stop the videos and explain them and set essays for the students to complete. Unlike a textbook, which only shows completed technical diagrams in economics, the videos showed how to construct the diagrams. This is exactly what students needed to comprehend to be capable of performing well in exams. I posted links of the videos up onto my digital platform, so the students could go back to them later in their own time. The videos were like having a classroom assistant that kept you organised. I could have drawn the diagrams freehand, which I occasionally did when the internet crashed, but the videos did the same job in a very clear and concise manner. This allowed me to comment more easily, as the diagrams were being constructed. If the students had tried to follow the videos without my analysis many of them would not have fully understood what was going on. The videos also helped to pace my lessons. I always had to keep pace with the syllabus so that the course would be finished in time for March in the senior year. If you overran then there would be no time for final revision, and this was essential for the students if they hoped to achieve the highest possible grades. The students seemed to appreciate my organised and methodical way of teaching and preparing them for exams. They always insisted exams were fair, and if they put in the effort then they had every chance to succeed.

Teaching IB business management is very different as apart from the finance section it is does not require the same linear thinking as economics. In many ways it is the opposite and requires lateral thinking. Business management as a subject is mainly definitions and huge amount of content to learn, but the trick is how to use that knowledge. It's not about listing off everything but more about critical thinking. In many ways it's like the skills required for english literature. Business management is mainly taught through case studies, so you need to work out who the main players or stakeholders are, what they are trying to achieve and what might prevent them from achieving their aims. You look for problems and solutions when reading the text. A good example is pricing strategies in marketing. You can't just list them all off to the examiner, you need to decide why the current pricing strategy being used in the case study is not appropriate, and to suggest a more appropriate pricing strategy giving reasons as to why you believe so. This is not about learning technical graphs and diagrams and shifting them around like in IB economics. I remember another time when talking about motivation using the real-life example of elite sport, particularly tennis. As a tennis fan I was talking about Federer and Nadal and how deeply motivated they both are, when one of the girls in the class asked, 'What about Andy Murray?' Slightly side-tracked, I replied that Murray was not in the same league, although still a great player. She then replied that she would tell Murray what I had said because he was her neighbour. Only at ACS did such conversations occur in my career. I hadn't said bad things about Murray at least, as I have huge respect for him as a two times Wimbledon champion. He's just not in the same league as Federer and Nadal as I said before.

As Cobham is the home of the Chelsea FC training ground, we taught many of the children of the Chelsea players at our school. The kids were often in the lower school, whilst I taught in the high school, but you would see Chelsea players from time to time on the campus. I recognised over the years Yossi Benayoun, Petr Cech, and Eden Hazard. I must have walked past countless others. I saw John Terry once down in Cobham high street. One of the lower school teachers knew Antonio Conte, so we knew before the general public when he quit Chelsea. In my first year at ACS, I even taught the brother-in-law of Roman Abramovich. I could have used Chelsea as my example for motivation in elite sport, but as a Tottenham fan I could never bring myself to do so. I preferred to stick with tennis.

For IB business management, just as for IB economics, I uploaded notes onto my Edmodo digital platform, and would run through PowerPoints in class, and have brief discussions. I'd then set case study assignments to test knowledge. This worked well in preparing the students for the exams, as it seemed to help them achieve good results. I never tried to stress the students with unexpected pop-up tests or quizzes, and I always made my classes relaxed and friendly, with everyone showing each other respect. The ACS students liked this mix of getting prepared and working for the exams, whilst not being constantly stressed by weekly tests. Like I previously said, I was not running GPA courses like the American Placement or AP courses, I was running IB courses preparing my students to peak at the end of two years for an end of course exam.

Business management was also only being taught to standard level at ACS when I arrived at the school. Many of the students had parents in business, and it was seen along with economics as a very important subject in the school. It was not an end of corridor A-level only subject on the fringes like in many state schools, at ACS my subject area was seen as very important. Parents and students began to push for higher level business management to be introduced, which I neither discouraged nor encouraged, I just said I was capable of teaching higher level if the management wanted me to. Eventually HL business management was introduced, and the numbers increased from a low point of about 30, to a high point of about 125. I was a cash cow at ACS earning them a great deal of profit, not that it would protect me.

Chasing up coursework was always a bit of a problem. Management wouldn't fail the kids, and the kids knew this so didn't take coursework deadlines seriously. Some would hand in their coursework right up until the time when it needed to be sent off to the IB. This would unfairly leave the teacher sometimes only hours to grade and process the marks, whilst the student had been given six months. It was always the maddest and busiest time of the year, but it always got completed. We weren't helping train the students to take responsibility, but money talked, and the school wanted the highest grades possible, so teacher coursework deadlines were just a huge bluff and meant nothing in the end. The only time a student almost missed the deadline for sending her coursework off to the exam board, was when she went to hand it in to me at 10.30pm one night in my later years at ACS when I worked in the dorm. Aisha accidentally hit the delete button instead of send and started crying. All I could do was walk off and tell her I needed it emailed to me by 8.30am the following morning, or the management for the first time ever would fail a student over coursework submission. Fortunately for the girl, her mum owned a company in Africa, and due to time differences with the UK the mum's business was open. Her mum then put her IT department onto retrieving the lost work of her darling princess. Miracles were performed, and the coursework was in my email inbox before 8.30am the following morning. At times like this it helped to be a rich kid. I then had two hours to grade and process the marks for management, and the girl passed. Who's to say she even wrote her own coursework. Many rich students no doubt paid someone to do their coursework, but you couldn't prove it. With the rise of artificial intelligence, I'm sure even more students these days don't do their own coursework. Coursework is no longer fit for purpose, and I personally would now advocate scrapping coursework. It would also make life a great deal easier for teachers, which should also be considered.

ACS was the only school I have ever been at where you were allowed to tutor students from the school. You couldn't tutor students from your own class, but you could tutor students from your colleague's class if they were struggling. You could make £40 per hour cash in hand tutoring. For some colleagues this was quite a significant extra earner. The school didn't mind as it boosted staff incomes without costing the school anything. Parents and students liked it as it allowed the problem of under-performance to be corrected by simply paying some money. As many of them were extremely wealthy, for them this was an easy solution. Everyone was happy, except for the taxman who missed out. I never did much tutoring as I liked my work life balance. I might take one student on for a few weeks in the run up to the summer exams some years, but that was about it. For me it was just some pocket money for a few nights out in London. I only ever tutored when approached and I did it more as a favour, as I didn't really like tutoring. Years later ACS stopped cash in hand tutoring. The taxman must have contacted the school saying they were liable for this tutoring on their premises, and everything had to be declared. At that point I stopped tutoring completely. Either I put the prices up to a point the parents refused to pay to cover the tax, or I effectively took a lower hourly rate which I wasn't prepared to do. There was no meeting of minds, which did not bother me as I never really liked tutoring like I keep saying. Students started to find unqualified cheap online tutors instead. For some teachers however losing the opportunity to tutor was a much bigger issue, and almost felt to them like a perk of the job had been removed.

Whilst at ACS my nan died at the grand old age of 95. I was very close to my nan; she was my partner in crime. We used to drink brandy together, recite poetry, play scrabble, and wind up my dear mum. It's my nan who taught me to get up after each setback, to dust myself down, and to go again. Indirectly her wartime lessons had been passed on to me, albeit in a somewhat diluted fashion. She had a big influence on me and losing her was another big loss. First my older brother, then my dad, and now my nan. The cycle of life can be very tough at times. My natural love of life, my friends, and my own family helped me to carry on, but I would never forget the lessons my nan had taught me. I'm pleased that she came up to visit me at ACS with my mum and younger brother Chris and saw my dorm room before she died. She was very proud of what I had achieved, and that meant the world to me.

When I returned to ACS a new office had been built in what had been the end of the corridor. I had lost my teaching room when I left, and I was put into the end of the corridor office. Over the next seven years I made this office my home from home. I spent hours once the seniors had left for study leave, sourcing and printing off quotes from the internet, which I then put up on the wall. Quotes from famous economists, business leaders, politicians, philosophers, historians, psychologists, and a few others. They sparked many an interesting conversation from my fellow teachers when they came into my office. My office was next to the photocopier, and I had my own coffee making machine. My friends and colleagues would often pop by for a coffee and a chat, whilst waiting for their photocopying. My office was at the very heart of the social studies department.

I decorated the wall behind my own desk with more personal images. Pictures of my family, and sporting icons such as John McEnroe, Ronnie O'Sullivan, Harry Kane, and Roger Federer. Pictures of places which I held dearly like St. Tropez in the South of France where I had gotten engaged years earlier, and some more quotes and inspirational messages. My entire office was an extension of me. When I walk into a classroom, I think displays are very important. They give a sense of the teacher, and if the teacher is fully invested in the students. A classroom with no wall displays often shows a teacher who isn't really that bothered about the kids. It's just a job and less of a vocation. The students can feel this and respond to it. Creating a positive classroom and learning environment is so important. I took this and applied it to my office, making it both a friendly and welcoming space. I also had office mates. Over my time I had many fun and insightful chats during morning break, free lessons, lunchtimes and after school. I had three different outgoing American women teachers in my office over the seven years, Cathy, Katie, and Mercedes. They were all amazing and kept me positive. As a Brit everything was ok and fine, but for my American friends everything was amazing and awesome. They were all so full of energy and positivity and I thrived off them. They loved my British wit and humour, and we all got on so well. I miss them all and have stayed in touch on and off with them. When I did finally leave ACS, I was happy that the last of the trio was still there to look after what had been my office and to take it on with that sense of welcoming everyone into my happy space. My other office mate of note was a history teacher called Graham. He was slightly older than me, very wise and knowledgeable and would often slow me down and make me think before I got too hot headed with the latest stupidity by management. We had many great discussions about history and Northern Ireland, and he became a very good friend of mine. He was another all-round great guy and I missed him when he left. He always had a twinkle in his eye and knew my mischievous ways of winding people up in a friendly way. He was always too wise to take my bait. At the very end there was also a South African younger female teacher called Simone who was also fun and straight talking. I liked her as well. I was so lucky to be surrounded by great teachers and friends. We had the best department at ACS, and I enjoyed it so much.

Two other great friends of note at ACS were Sean the geography teacher and Brian who was in the english department. Along with Cathy from the office, the trio came a couple of times to Belfast to visit me where we all had a veritable blast. Often teachers would proclaim they would come to visit me in Belfast, but the Americans often followed through and did it. I love this American positivity, something which we Brits lack at times. The four of us then formed what we called the Pub Club which was to become the forerunner to my later Phoenix Club.

I was also very fond of Keith an ageing punk rocker with a cutting sense of humour, a quick wit, and a strong sense of sarcasm. He was another english teacher. Then there was Jonathan the head of english who loved whiskey, music, literature and playing devil's advocate. He was always one of my favourites. Yet another character was Kurak, a Canadian professor of philosophy who was out of place in a high school teaching TOK. You'd often find him listening to Belgian choral music wishing he was elsewhere. I should also mention Westy, an anglicised Welshman. Chris was always very supportive and friendly, sometimes driving me to the airport, and he was the first to phone me to see if I was ok later when ACS threatened me with redundancy. ACS was my home from home, it had become my second family. I was surrounded by all my friends in the high school. It's a shame the same couldn't be said of the senior management in the end.

My now HOD Adam used to run an annual History trip to Ypres and the World War 1 trenches. I had been to Ypres many years before and it had always left a mark. All the names on the Menin Gate were just those of the soldiers who had perished in the Battle of Ypres. World War 1 was horrific and should never be forgotten. I had more recently been to the World War 2 cemeteries in Normandy whilst I had been at Wallace, but I really wanted to go back to the WW1 trenches and Ypres. The trip was a day long marathon; I couldn't even get down to ACS in time for the early start from North London, so I had to arrange to sleep on the dorm for the night. We'd set off early on coaches, make the Eurotunnel, drive to the trenches, go to Ypres and the museum, and then make it back to the Eurotunnel and back to Blighty just in time for bed. I went on the trip twice, and both times it didn't go smoothly. We either got delayed at the Channel Tunnel and barely had time to eat all day, or the coach drivers got lost and couldn't find their way around to specific booked museums. I was the unlucky mascot of the trip, as it ran smoother the other years when I didn't go. One image I shan't forget was that of another teacher called Michael pulling his clanking trolley case over the cobbled streets of Ypres. He had rushed through the museum, found a store that sold Belgian beer and had stocked up. He was smiling from ear to ear, extremely happy with himself. Different people had different reasons for going on the trip, I like Belgian beer, but I was primarily there to see the WW1 trenches and the Menin Gate. Since Brexit many educational trips to Europe have stopped. It's now too much hassle and paperwork for the teachers, so many trips no longer go. This is also true of the Ypres trip. It's such a shame as these trips are so beneficial for the students. Covid only compounded the problem, and trips are becoming fewer and fewer. Residential trips are fast becoming a thing of the past, with just some domestic day trips still hanging on.

I also went on a day trip to the HMS Victory, which brought back fond childhood memories, a trip to Chessington World of Adventure and an encounter with The Wave of Terror with my good friend Peter, and several football supporters' trips to Fulham's Craven Cottage and Crystal Palace's Selhurst Park with Chris the Welsh history teacher. I also used to go on the theatre trips to the West End shows with my friends Cathy and Brian. The tickets were heavily discounted, and a coach picked us up and dropped us off right next to the dorm in the main ACS campus car park. I viewed the theatre trips as a huge perk. I got to see The Lion King, Phantom of the Opera, Chicago, and Les Misérables. I should have gone to more.

Getting involved in trips adds to the community spirit of teaching within schools. You see the students outside of the classroom and get time to talk more with your teaching colleagues. They are fun, but also help deepen the bonds which when back at school helps to provide a greater sense of community. It's a shame that many managers see trips as an insurance risk and would almost rather they didn't take place. Little by little schools are being strangled by management covering themselves from potential legal prosecution. It's sad, and the losers are the students themselves who get fewer and fewer opportunities to experience trips and a wide variety of extra-curricular activities. We are teaching a generation of students who experience life more in the virtual world and less in the real world, than compared to students of even just twenty years ago.

I also ran the chess club and table tennis club whilst at ACS. I always got heavily involved in the schools I spent the most time in. If my career had just been a long list of schools I had only subbed in, then it would not have been so fulfilling. Northwood, Wallace, and ACS were the beating heart of my career, ACS in particular.

We were often used at ACS for invigilation, or proctoring as the Americans call it, for the end of year exams in the gym. The interior walls of the gym were made up of light blue painted bricks. Invigilation is one of the most boring tasks assigned to teachers. At ACS I tried to find ways of making the drudgery more interesting. You'd wander about, then sit still for a while, then wander about some more. I on one occasion tried to count the total number of bricks making up the gymnasium walls. There were thousands and thousands of them, and I kept losing count. In the end I think there were just over 28000 bricks, but I could be a little wrong. This is how dull invigilation can be. The only times when there was any slight amusement was when you were invigilating with some of your friends. You might wander past each other and whisper some inane joke, or maybe make funny hand signs from the back of the hall. Our favourite was invigilation Pac-Man. You'd move around through the rows of desks and try to corner your friend, or it would be their turn to try and do the same to you. One on one invigilation Pac-Man was nearly impossible, but two on one invigilation Pac-Man and it was game on. I remember once cornering Adam my HOD with the help of Jonathan the head of english. The students never even knew we were playing the game.

Graduation was always a huge event at ACS. The seniors after the exams would all wear academic gowns and mortarboards for the graduation ceremony. The teachers would all be in academic gowns, and the parents would be in the audience. High school graduation is an American tradition. In the UK we graduate from university, so at first, I found the whole idea slightly strange, especially as it only meant you had finished high school and had nothing to do with passing any exams. At first, I thought it ludicrous that lazy students who had probably failed once the results came out, were swanning around and lapping all the adulation up. I did however grow to enjoy the occasion over the years. Marketing also enjoyed it as it gave all the fee-paying parents a lovely day out and provided a public opportunity to feel proud about their children. After all the speeches and moving the tassels from one side of the mortarboard to the other to denote the precise moment of graduation, everyone retired outside to the fountain area. The marquis tents were ready with champagne flutes and enticing delicacies for everyone to consume. Everyone mingled, chatting away merrily, and then the moment of the hat toss came. The seniors would all gather in front of the fountain for a group photo, and then all toss their mortarboards up into the air at the same time. Parents proudly took photos and teachers drank free champagne. Afterwards the students would all start to disperse to go out for lunches with their parents or to go to a graduation party. One year I was fortunate enough along with my friends Cathy, Brian, and Svetlana to be invited to a graduation party. It took place in the garden of one of my students called Angel. The same student who lived across the street from Andy Murray. The house was a mansion, it had a sweeping staircase and an indoor swimming pool. The mum greeted us, was extremely friendly and thanked us for all the hard work we had done in helping her daughter. We bumped into Keith and a few other teachers including my head of year Luke, a fun Australian teacher who had also been invited. I danced, chatted, drank limoncello and had a wonderful time. It was always interesting to get a glimpse into the lives of the wealthy students. It added to your own education and understanding of the world and helped to better understand the students in your classroom.

Although I was perfectly capable and qualified to teach both IB economics and IB business management, from a marketing point of view the school was very keen to send me on the IB training courses. This would allow both myself and the school to say to parents and students that I was IB qualified. It would give me more protection from potential complaining parents, so I didn't mind being sent on the courses. I especially didn't mind when it meant I was being sent all expenses paid to Paris for the IB business management course, and to Berlin for the IB economics course. The Paris course was being run in a hotel around the corner from La Bastille, where my younger brother used to live. I had lived in Paris in the past as well and spoke french. This was not an adventure but was more like a nostalgic trip back to Paris. On the course you got to meet teachers from other IB schools and authors of the IB textbooks who were running the course. You exchanged resources, learnt things you already knew, and had a couple of fun nights out with the other teachers. In Paris I took the lead and showed everyone the bars in the local area. One guy from the Czech Republic spent the night telling me about the Velvet Revolution and was mightily impressed that I could nearly drink as much as him. Berlin on the other hand was different. I neither speak German, nor had been to Berlin before. This was more like an adventure. I had always wanted to see Berlin and Checkpoint Charlie. We had a couple of great nights out as a group of teachers down the bars in east Berlin besides the river, swapped resources, and all went back to our respective schools with a spring in our steps. That was all soon to change. ACS lost customers due to Brexit, overspent on opening a new dorm, and lost further customers due to Covid. It expected to lose even more due to the war initiated by Russia against Ukraine. This loss of revenue panicked ACS and everything became about cost cutting. My latest IB staff training was not about being sent away anywhere to meet other teachers, but instead to sit online on and off over a six-week period and complete assignments. It was terrible, no fun, a lot of work, and taught me nothing I didn't already know. I didn't get to swap resources with other teachers and all in all it was a more demotivating experience than a motivating one. Management didn't care, they could tick a box to say I was trained, and they had saved money. This cost cutting was replicated everywhere throughout the school. It became harder to order textbooks, photocopying was more monitored, staff in the dorm and elsewhere were reduced, and eventually the school made some redundancies. This was all a very far cry from the school I had first joined where money had been no object. When I first joined ACS staff were given champagne at the end of term, there were more gifts admittedly more from the parents, and budgets were all round more generous. Now ACS was becoming mean and cost cutting. Staff were now being seen as the major expense rather than as the major asset. Older more expensive and more experienced staff who had once been good for the marketing image were now more out of favour. In favour were cheaper, more pliable and tech savvy younger staff. The state sector approach of recruitment was beginning to take hold in the private sector. It was becoming more about cost cutting rather than quality and experience. I hoped all this would eventually get better, but it just got steadily worse post 2016 and the Brexit result.

I hate Brexit. As an economics teacher it is madness. Its consequences would impact upon us all. First there was The Entitlement Framework, and then there was Brexit. Politicians have a lot to answer for, especially Conservative ones who put into place policies to help corporations and the wealthy. Policies which worsen equality and living standards for the general population. Cost cutting could be replaced by lower profits and dividend payments to shareholders. Staff could be treated as an asset instead of as a cost. It's a choice, and British management do not choose staff wellbeing over shareholder profits, and Conservative governments collude with corporate managers to prioritise corporate profits over the workforce who help create the profits.

I was beginning to get tired of commuting across London every day, and I was beginning to think I couldn't allow myself to get too comfortable. Joanna had provided me with a lifeline and a way of working in London, by letting me stay at her house in Finchley. If she ever moved, I would be in trouble, so I decided to move on first. I'm glad I did because a couple of years later she retired and moved from London to Malta and sold her house. I decided to join the dormitory. I had stayed a couple of nights before when going on the Belgian trip to Ypres. A couple of my friends were already on the dorm and were persuading me to join, and then a vacancy came up. One of the teachers was leaving the dorm, I applied to replace her, and suddenly I was now a member of the ACS dorm. I now had a second job alongside my primary job of teaching in the high school. It meant I had to work two evenings a week, and about seven weekends a year away from home, but it also meant that I no longer had to commute over 24 hours a week. I would wake up in my dorm accommodation three minutes' walk from my office in the high school and could get up every morning at 7.25am instead of 5.15am. Free food was also part of the deal, and I could get free breakfast, lunch, and dinner every day in the school canteen. Breakfast and dinner were always both highly sociable where you would sit around with the other dorm staff and chat about football, politics, or anything else of interest that day. The laundry was done every week and in the early years of the dorm we also had a cleaner. I was tired, and I think joining the dorm allowed me to cope for longer with working away from home in London. In many ways the dorm made my life easier and enriched my time at ACS.

My first two years in the dorm were in what we as staff now call the old dorm. I started my dorm shifts with Leigh, a New Zealand science teacher who kindly showed me the ropes. We made a great team and I have great memories of working with Leigh and his wife Sue on the dorm. The old dorm had red brick walls, two floors, and students were two to a room. It had a homely feel about it. The dorm made my life easier; it made it easier for me to keep up with the ever-increasing workload in the high school. The time I saved each day on the commute across London I could now use instead to complete the new obligatory web-based Safety Cloud health and safety training; or use the time to populate Edmodo my original digital learning platform, or PowerSchool Learning my new digital learning platform. I could use the time to mark exams or write reports. At this point the duties in the dorm were straightforward, although the occasional weekend duty hours were very long and tedious. As a resident tutor you were just expected to monitor the kids, to get to know them, and to report more serious matters onto the dorm house parents who ran the day-to-day business of the dorm. This suited me well. I was busy at home at weekends with my family, and busy during the week already in the high school. We'd sit down in the evening and monitor the corridors on study hall for a couple of hours, then for the rest of the shift mingle in the common rooms with the students, often chatting and watching them play table tennis. We watched many memorable football matches in the dorm, created a bond with other dormers both staff and students alike, and were part of an extended family. Back in the high school, dormers would all give each other a passing nod in the corridors. In the classroom there was a deeper bond between dormers. As one of the few teachers in the dorm, this made me more popular than before in the high school, as now all the dorm kids looked out for me as well as they regarded me as one of them. We were the dorm.

We took the dormers on many day trips at weekends. I remember going to Leeds Castle, The Imperial War Museum, and The British Museum. Other times we went zorbing or paintballing. We also used to go to the pantomime each year with the dorm kids. International kids didn't always fully understand the British tradition of pantomimes, but they still seemed to love them. Dick Whittington, Puss in Boots, or Peter Pan, it made little difference. The auditorium would always erupt with cries of laughter and "he's behind you."

The staff after shift would just go to their rooms and watch TV or go to sleep. Joining the dorm at first is a cultural sledgehammer. You have given up your freedom and are locked into your room. For a freedom loving fun person I found this difficult. Fortunately, I started with another fun-loving teacher from Turkey called Adile who felt the same, so in those early weeks I had someone who understood. I decided to start work on a project, I decided to try and get other staff out of their rooms and to socialise more. I started with my old pal Mr Lee the legend of the dorm, and to try and spread it from there. When you have two people, and then three, and then four, soon others start to join in, and this is how it evolved. We soon had some semi regular whiskey nights going, where we'd sit up and chat, and just chill out after a long day's work. We rarely drank that much as we had to get up the next day to go and teach. Whilst this was going on ACS was also in the middle of constructing a new dorm. They were hoping to cash in on a lucrative market and to make more profits. It was just before Brexit. My whole project finally came together on the last night in the old dorm. It was the end of June and the students had left for the end of term, and on our return to school in the August we would be moving to the new dorm. For some it was very emotional as they had been on the old dorm for years. We found some old hats, I handed out nicknames, and we sat around outside drinking, laughing, and singing until the early hours. Some of us stayed up and saw the sunrise. This became the infamous plaza party and where the Phoenix Club was born. Why the Phoenix Club? It's because the phoenix always rises from the ashes, and it can never be kept down. It felt a bit like the journey I had taken throughout my teaching career. Always rising to new challenges and new schools, and never being kept down. It just seemed like the right name at the time. It was a positive statement and testament to the fact that the Phoenix Club once born would forever endure.

We took the spirit of the plaza party over to the new dorm with us. The new dorm was officially named Woodlands, whilst the old dorm was officially named Fields. The staff rooms were on the lower ground floor in an L shape, with no access into the dorm itself. We were our own little private community. It was never planned, but The Phoenix Club probably became my greatest legacy at ACS. One of the staff called Dave had been the head of sports, and he loved both teambuilding and whiskey. He named me Lord Centurion, whilst I named him Coach. Pete the legendary anchor of the dorm was Grandpappy, and some of the other Phoenix names over the next 5 years were Benny, Blondie, Naughty Nipper, Brew Master, Hollywood, Lucky, Helen of Troy, Scarface, Tinkerbell, Xena, Big Jock, and Pixie. There were others that have escaped me. Everyone helped pick their own names, and they were all a bit of fun intended to increase camaraderie. We had many soirees, BBQs, Christmas gatherings, and late nights especially on training days when the students weren't on campus. We would have afternoon teas outside each other's rooms, and weekly coffee trips down to Cobham. Sometimes Shabs another teacher would drive us down to Cobham in her BMW, and we'd arrive in style. In my last couple of years, we also started having soirees behind Brew Master's sheds. He would gather wood and make a fire, project up a movie, and pass around his homebrew. Other times we would all just listen to music and sing songs instead of watching movies. It took me back to my time in the scouts when I was a child. Campfires, good company, homebrew, and an outdoor cinema. It's hard to beat. My favourite night was when we watched National Lampoon's Animal House. "Thank-you, God." It's not a film that has aged well, but in the right company it is still funny. Other soirees were back in the social room up by the staff accommodation. We sometimes just watched football on the TV, other times we just gathered chatting and drinking until late. It was like a second coming of university halls of residence. On a Tuesday and a Thursday night after shift I would sit outside with just Peter and chat and look up at the stars. I called these Phoenix Nights. Others dropped in to talk to us, but for five years it was always just me and Pete. You get to know someone very well after spending so much time together, and Pete is very special to me. During my time at Woodlands dorm, I also went through a short period when I used to get up early. I'd either go to the gym, walk around the athletics track, or more often walk around the woods that surrounded the campus. I love walking, and the early morning magical mists across the heath and on the river always made me feel I'd already done something worthwhile before even starting school. Sometimes I'd get lucky and get offered a Turkish coffee by Adile, one of my good friends in the dorm that was often sitting outside the social room just as I was going for breakfast. There is nothing like a strong coffee to get you going in the morning. She'd then sometimes read the coffee sludge to tell each other's fortune. It was all just a bit of made-up fun, using the coffee sludge to try and visualise images and then to make up a story.

In my last year we got a boost from Naughty Nipper the monster from Oz and Xena the Welsh Warrior Princess and Woodlands team leader. Instead of being a bad last year with a tyrant new houseparent, the new house staff made it one of the very best. Nipper and Xena were such a laugh, and they added an extra boost to The Phoenix Club. On my leaving do, staff both present and old came out to give me a send-off. I was presented with a Phoenix Club Lord Centurion whiskey glass, whiskey rocks, and an expensive £120 bottle of whiskey amongst other gifts. It was another evening to remember, and there was so much warmth and happiness that night that I realised that I'd had a hugely positive impact on the dorm staff wellbeing. I also knew it was my time to move on and leave the Phoenix Club in the hands of the younger newer staff and the last couple of old timers still left, yet once a dormer, always a dormer.

After Brexit came Covid and a change of management. The new head of campus was a disaster for the teaching staff, the very worst type of manager possible. He was an autocratic bully, with little to offer except some old ideas that he brought with him from the British system. International schools are very different to British schools and have a different culture. Imposing British school systems just weakens the uniqueness of an international school, whilst still not making it like a British school such as Charterhouse. The new bully boy started to centralise power, in the deluded belief that he was great. He wasn't looking for engagement, just compliance. He started to bully the HODs, and to increase the workload. Staff became less happy, and the morale dropped. This is all whilst Covid hit, and suddenly ACS had changed. I still loved the social studies department and all my students, but the corporation was cost cutting and treating staff poorly. This goes against all the motivation theories I had taught my students in business management over the years. Some staff in the past had been unfairly accused and marched off campus. One friend called Sam who was the teachers union representative had been bullied by previous management to the extent that he became severely stressed. He soon afterwards got a form of cancer and died. After Sam we never had a union representative for the teaching staff that was recognised by the ACS management. The senior management didn't like trade unions. I never got over what happened to Sam, and I never forgave the ACS senior management. In my humble opinion their bullying had triggered his illness.

It appeared to me that Barny the head of campus in my later years at ACS had been employed amongst other things to cut staffing costs post Brexit. He soon employed a head of high school called Fred, and some of us laughed and called it The Flintstones. Who's next? We wondered, Betty, Wilma and then Bam Bam? It was however no laughing matter. Fred was fine and turned out to be a very pleasant person, but he was being dictated to by Barny who appeared to be getting frustrated. Covid was delaying his plans, and he wanted to make himself look good by saying look at all the wonderful changes he was making. His changes in my opinion were merely mediocre at best, and extremely damaging at worst for the morale of the teaching staff, and by extension I would argue for the wellbeing of the entire school community. Never have I had so little respect for a manager. Barny had an inflated ego with a lack of empathy for others. He made it clear it was his way or the highway and set about dictating to the teaching faculty to force through his desired changes, whilst maybe also hoping to drive away older more expensive, more experienced, and less pliable staff who disagreed with him. It was my misfortune to be unfairly caught up at the wrong time in his sights.

ACS announced cutbacks would be taking place, my HOD said I was the heart of his department and that I was safe. I had increased student numbers on my courses, I had been flexible over the years, I had good results, I hit deadlines, and I engaged and offered ways to improve. The school was on lockdown, I was back home in Belfast delivering distance learning and the phone rang. I'd been selected for potential redundancy. You cannot be serious! My HOD Adam had not been told, and his opinion had not been sought. I did the rounds and found out that only three teaching staff in the high school had been targeted. Two that had been on the management hit list for a while, and me. I had only a month earlier at the insistence of my wife, complained to Barny the head of campus about being bullied by the dorm management for choosing to go home to my family in Belfast for lockdown. The dorm management had wanted me to stay on the dorm for a lockdown rota, which had not yet been announced when I had gone home. I was caught in a crossfire between my wife and the dorm management, but I had no real choice; I couldn't get stuck at school throughout Covid away from my family. Borders were closing, fear was rampant, and soon travel between England and Northern Ireland would be prohibited. I was always going to choose my family; it was a no brainer. Anyhow, the head of high school had already given me permission to go home, so I hadn't perceived there to be any problem as the high school was my main employer rather than the dorm. The reward in the end it seemed for complaining about being bullied was not to be listened to but to be sacked instead. I had dared to stand up for myself, and that it seemed was not to be tolerated by senior management who viewed it as a direct challenge to their authority. It was nothing of the sort, I loved ACS, but I had to go home to help look after my sons during Covid lockdown, and furthermore the head of high school had given me permission to go.

A fabricated subjective points system was then constructed by management with the aim to get rid of me. It was utterly outrageous. This was a base betrayal of a loyal and effective long time serving member of staff by senior management and was a direct attack on my family. I was in total shock, but I told all my faculty friends who quickly rallied around me. The management by their own system however had not done their homework properly, they targeted me as a business management teacher, and forgot I could also teach IB economics. They were so incompetent that they couldn't even hit a stationary mark that had been ambushed. I was allowed one person in the online meeting to discuss the redundancy, so I contacted my HOD who was raging. He attended with me. I didn't want a solicitor or a union rep, I wanted to stay at ACS so I brought my HOD and good friend Adam, who should have been in the meeting anyway. The meeting started, I put over my points, they ignored me, then my HOD repeated my points. Immediately management back tracked. Adam my HOD has been at the school nigh on 30 years and is highly respected. A new meeting was called, and they told me I was now safe and that another teacher would be made redundant instead. I could stay at the school and teach economics. I love economics, it was my main subject at university. It had all worked out for me in the end, it seemed as if my good luck was holding. The redundancy process was all a poorly managed farce. It should never have happened, and it dented my loyalty to the school. My wife wanted me to immediately resign and stay in Belfast, but out of loyalty to my HOD Adam I decided to return to ACS for two more years and to bed down the new IB economics syllabus. Adam had been my human shield and I wanted to repay him and show him my appreciation by completing one last job for him before I could no longer resist the need to go back home to Belfast.

These were to be the Covid years. A mixture of lockdowns and teaching from my home in Belfast on Zoom, to travelling through fear infested empty airports each week to fly back and forth to work. The school implemented a one-way system around the corridors, everyone wore face masks and used hand gel, and no one went to the staffroom. I gave up my teaching room to a member of staff who was scared, and I was housed for the year in the teaching room of my good friend and brother in economics, Rob my Californian guru. I knew I was in my final years at ACS, so I'm so happy I spent that year with Robert in his room. He had a back office and would pop his head out and hand me coffees. During break we would hang out, as with the one-way system it was difficult to go anywhere. The Covid years could have been very isolating but in the high school just sharing the room meant you always had a buddy at hand. Classes were strange with some students in the classroom and others on Zoom, but somehow step by step we chipped away and carried on making progress. I was now only teaching IB economics, and back to my passion at university. I also had Pete in the dorm, who lived in the room next to mine, so between Rob and Pete, and a few others, I kept my sanity. We all helped each other, and the initial Covid year at ACS passed. I think I got Covid myself twice being on the front line. A couple of times I experienced finding it hard to breathe but I had a mortgage to pay and had little choice but to soldier on. We nearly all got Covid eventually. We were all dispensable key workers without the luxury of hiding safely away in our homes. Covid killed too many people that didn't need to die.

And then at Christmas of the following year I decided I'd had enough of the senior management. They would never get better and would only get worse. My wife was telling me she wanted me to come home, and I wanted to get home before my sons left school and went to university. Rob my Californian econ guru was also going to be leaving ACS at the end of the academic year. I got a job as a sixth form study supervisor in a grammar school back in Belfast and handed in my notice. I stayed until just after St. Patrick's Day, collected in all the coursework, marked the mock exams, and finished the syllabus. I left two weeks before the end of the Easter term. I had bedded in the new IB economics syllabus for Adam my HOD, the students were now just revising and didn't truly need me anymore, and I left to go home to Belfast and my family. Pete drove me to Heathrow, via one last full English breakfast, he gave me a parting hug as he dropped me off, and then I was gone. I was extremely sad to leave ACS and all my friends, but it was my time to leave, and I left on my own terms with a good reference from my HOD. I had spent all those years to get back to where I'd been before I had left Wallace, as a respected full time permanent member of staff, and now I was losing it all again. I'd made the journey twice now in teaching. I'd learnt so much, and met so many interesting people, but it was now time to prioritise my family. I had no regrets. I arranged to come back a couple of months later to the ACS graduation to see all my senior students again, and all my teaching friends for one last Phoenix Night, but then that would be it. My time at ACS was over. I'd stay in touch with my friends, but I probably wouldn't go back to the campus again after graduation. It was the end of an era.

I'd been away from Belfast for just over ten years, and in that time, I'd done about 750 flights. I was tired and I needed a rest.

Grosvenor Mixed Grammar

I left ACS on the Friday as a teacher of 27 years and started on the Monday at Grosvenor Grammar School as a member of the non-teaching staff. Grosvenor's claim to fame is that it is the school that George Best the football legend went to after passing his 11-plus. As a grammar school Grosvenor played rugby and not football, so George eventually left Grosvenor to go to a nearby non-grammar school where he could play football with his friends, and the rest is history as they say. On arrival at Grosvenor, I had three weeks to get the lower sixth focussed on studying for their exams before their Easter holidays, and then a couple of weeks more after Easter. Everyone was nice. The management were pleasant. I was back in a school rather than in a private business. George the cleaner dropped by my room every afternoon to give me the East Belfast gossip. My wife dropped me off in the morning, my father-in-law picked me up in the afternoon. I got to spend evenings and weekends with my family. Life was easier. I did however miss my friends from ACS. The pay was much less, the job almost felt like semi-retirement, but it still seemed the right move. I'd come home. I'd come full circle. I wondered how long it would last. The Queen's Platinum Jubilee was fast approaching; I could wait at least I thought until after the jubilee before I needed to start thinking again about my longer-term future.

Reflections

Whatever had happened to The Cayman Islands or some other destination both exotic and warm? That would have been my next obvious career move. What had happened? I had chosen my family over my career, and I had made the right decision. I'd come home. There was nothing left to prove or achieve in my teaching career.

I have learnt a great deal. Teaching as a profession is upside down and back to front. It should be about the teachers in the classroom with the students, and for the teachers it still is, however management often have different ideas. For them it is about league tables and budgets. It is about endless administration and tracking data, which take up the time that should be spent on lesson preparations and marking. Management should be the administrative back up to the professional teachers, instead they have become bosses who often treat professional teachers like factory floor workers. They too often interfere, telling the professional teachers how they should teach. Teaching as a profession is not respected like it should be, and the professionals have lost control of their own profession. The workload and stress levels are often not worth the level of pay received, and many new teachers quit within the first few years and many older teachers retire early. Yet many teachers remain. This is because despite some poor management, despite the lack of respect and increasing workload, despite poor pupil behaviour in many schools, and despite the poor pay for what teachers do, for many teachers it is still about helping our students. It is a passion, a purpose, a vocation, a calling if you like. It is a privilege to help the young generation. The reward is not counted in monetary terms, rather it is counted in human terms. Teaching allows you to remain true to who you are, and it helps nourish your soul. For all the barriers and difficulties, I can't imagine I would rather have had any other career. In the end I learnt that I was born to be a teacher. No amount of training or experience can create this, some people are natural born teachers, and we live for what we do.

Would I recommend teaching to anyone else? Yes, most certainly, but only if it's what you truly love and you need to find the right school for you as they are all different. As I reflect on my twenty-seven years to date in teaching, spread across twenty schools teaching fifteen different subjects, I can honestly say that I have seen more than nearly any other teacher I have met. I've also never met a teacher who flew to work every week for over ten years. I have enjoyed my life as a teacher, and although I'm still in a classroom in a supervisory role here at Grosvenor, maybe it's time for a new generation of younger teachers to take over. A generation of teachers fit to teach the iPad generation of students. The world is fast changing as we progress through the twenty first century, and my first cohort of students back in 1995 by now are probably the parents of students in 2022. I am not fully of the technological world, but also of a world where human relationships and real-world experiences matter most. I am starting to feel a little tired, I am beginning to feel that semi-retirement and just being with my family is where I now belong.

After a brief rest, I may step up again to another permanent job in teaching. Maybe I'm just a bit tired and will feel differently in a few months' time.

Then suddenly a job teaching business studies came up in of all places at Grosvenor, less than 2 months after starting work at the school. It was a freaky coincidence as teaching jobs in business studies and economics are extremely rare in Belfast. Was this a sign? Either way I decided to apply and see what would happen. Either fate had me ear marked to go back into teaching, or fate was telling me it was over, and I was effectively semi-retired. If I couldn't get the job in the school I was already working in, then I wouldn't get a permanent full time teaching job anywhere in Northern Ireland. I'm still waiting as I write these words to see what is going to happen. Maybe I haven't finished with teaching yet, maybe I have.

Then a teaching opportunity suddenly also came up in Istanbul. Somewhere both warm and slightly exotic, where you can also earn enough money in a prestigious international school to save for your retirement. The cost-of-living crisis is growing in my mind. I feel I would need to go abroad if I am to earn enough to finally pay off all my debts and keep up with all the soaring bills. It seems wrong that you need to go abroad as a classroom teacher to earn a better salary, and that you can't earn enough in the UK to save significant amounts or buy a house anymore in many parts of the country. Many younger teachers are coming to the same conclusion and are heading abroad to pursue their careers in countries that offer both better pay and conditions. I am at a crossroads again, with choices to make. It seems I still do not know what the long-term future holds. When I search my soul and am true to myself however, I still feel the need to be at home with my family. Maybe Istanbul will have to wait.

If I don't get the full-time teaching job at Grosvenor, I might just go supply teaching again in Belfast and give up being a sixth form study supervisor. I need to earn more money to help pay my mortgage, plus I was born to teach not merely just to baby sit classes. Maybe I just need to take a deep breath, to lift myself up once more and to go again. To start on a third journey in teaching. I've already completed two journeys, from building myself up in my early career and teaching at Wallace, to re-building my career and teaching at ACS Cobham. I was at another crossroads in my career it seemed. Maybe Istanbul or somewhere else abroad would be a better fit in 3 years' time once my kids have grown up and gone to university. That perhaps could be my final chapter in teaching. I could save for my retirement then, whilst at the same time expand upon my classroom and life experiences. My story I feel has yet to fully finish. I'm neither ready, nor financially able to retire just yet. There's still some life in the classroom left in me. It's where I still belong for a few more years yet it seems. It looks like 3 years of supply teaching in Belfast and then maybe a few years teaching abroad. I think at that point I'd finally be ready to retire. Finally, ready to walk away from my life in the classroom.

My thanks go to all the students who have passed through my classroom doors, to my teaching colleagues, and to my wife who has supported me through all the ups and downs over the years. It has been a long and rewarding yet also difficult road, which was more about the journey than the destination. I am about to commence a new journey whatever that might be and have much to look forward to. Life is short, I intend to enjoy my new chapter and all those that follow to the fullest. Life is for living; blink and it passes you by.

Phoenix Rising

A Life in the classroom - Memoirs of teaching by Martyn Agass

April / May 2022

Extra Time 2022 – 2024

Campbell College All Boy's Grammar

And then the day before pupils went back to school at the end of August, Campbell College phoned me up. Could I please go in the next day as a member of staff had unexpectedly not returned from sick leave? I was to be parachuted into a crisis with less than 24 hours-notice. It appears there is no rest for the wicked. Campbell College is one of the most prestigious schools in Belfast. CS Lewis of Narnia fame is an ex-pupil, and the lamp post in the famous book The Lion the Witch and the Wardrobe is in the school grounds. The walls are wood panelled adorned with plaques of the names of past students who represented the school in all manner of sports. The floors are red tiled, and there are sweeping stone staircases, with some stone carving, stained glass windows, and portraits scattered about. It all feels like a time capsule of the British Empire dated back to the turn of the twentieth century. It's the closest I have ever come to teaching at Hogwarts, the school of Harry Potter fame. The staff are all very friendly and happy to work at such a prestigious school. The building and the expansive grounds have a powerful effect on everyone at the school.

Campbell also has a boarding house with many international students. After my time at ACS teaching international students, and having spent many years in boarding, this all adds to my sense of this being a school I could stay at.

Campbell seems to be a good fit at this stage and could become yet another significant chapter in my teaching career, or it could just become another interesting job for however long it lasts. It all depends on how long Campbell decide they need me for. Again, time will tell, but it has already called me back into the classroom to teach once more. You just never know what lies around the corner. Right now, I have been re-invented yet again, and this time as a Victorian schoolmaster with a smile. Who would have thought this when I was at Grosvenor and being under-utilised as a sixth form study supervisor.

And then the Queen died in my second week at Campbell College. Only a few months ago it had been her Platinum Jubilee. The country was in shock and mourning. A new era was upon us after so many years of stability under Queen Elizabeth II. She had been the rock and anchor of the nation since the post war period right up until the digital age. God rest her soul. We were now entering the age of King Charles III. So much change in so short a time, but if anyone can offer both continuity and stability it's King Charles. God save the king.

It seems that Act III of my career might be starting after Act I ended with Wallace and Act II ended with ACS. Act III might be starting with Campbell. I need to find the energy and build myself up again for a third time.

Larne High School Mixed Comprehensive

The phone rang, and the principal of Larne High School offered me work for the rest of the academic year. It would be teaching mainly science and maths, with health and social care a BTEC award subject. Campbell could not guarantee me long term work, and the principal of Larne High was an old colleague and friend of my wife Lorraine. The cost-of-living crisis was worsening, so I decided to take the offer. I would be on my travels yet again. I said my goodbyes to Campbell and started travelling up to Larne every day with Lorraine. My commute had become so much easier and cheaper than when I commuted for over 10 years to London. Campbell was not to be.

I had left the state sector in 2011 when I started working in London. My main experience of working in state schools had been during the years of the Labour government from 1997 to 2010. On my return after 12 years of a Conservative government, I was quite shocked by what I saw. I have seen many schools over the years, but there was no denying the 12 years of austerity in the public sector and chronic under funding. At Larne High, class sizes were bigger than had been the case in the late 1990s. Workload and admin were also greater. Not only that but real pay had declined by 20% since the Conservatives had come to power. The kids' behaviour had also declined. I'm sure the after-effects of Covid had something to do with this, as did the fact that the youngsters now had been born into a world of mobile phones and computers. They are all addicted to social media and their devices and seem to lack the attention span to listen and study. Teaching as a career had changed for the worse. A combination of government underfunding of public services, Covid, poor pay, and social changes with regards to mobile phones and the need for instant gratification.

I quite liked the idea of teaching something different again. I was going to be triple outside of my comfort zone. Teaching more junior school than senior school, teaching poorly behaved children, and teaching subjects that weren't my own. Science would prove the trickiest as running practical lessons was not viable for insurance purposes. With the teaching of all the 3 science subjects plus health and social care, I would now be up to 22 schools and 19 subjects throughout my career.

The staff at Larne High were very welcoming and friendly. The headmaster was a friendly and decent human being. He was why I went to the school. After the bullyboy headmaster at ACS, I was looking for a boss who treated people with the respect they deserved. I wanted to work for someone that I both liked and respected. The kids at Larne High though were most challenging. They often had a low opinion of themselves and of the school. I would often spend time trying to build up their confidence. However, there was a proportion of the pupils that would just not be quiet and listen. They were determined not to work and learn and made teaching and learning more stressful for everyone. I just carried on and got through this and slowly started to earn the respect of many of the pupils. There were some that you would never reach, they were too closed and too far gone before they ever entered my classroom. Sometimes it just felt like babysitting so the parents could go out to work, rather than trying to teach the next generation so they could better themselves.

Teaching assistants were also everywhere. I was not used to this. I was not quite sure what as the teacher I was supposed to do with teaching assistants. I decided to just carry on as normal as if they weren't there and let them do their thing. Some were helpful, some were less helpful. The explosion in the number of teaching assistants has been a large change in state sector schools. They obviously cost the school, and I can only assume are deemed essential to helping students with learning issues. From my point of view however, I could happily teach a class with no teaching assistants. What would be more helpful would be to employ more teachers so class sizes could be reduced.

Larne High was a mad place. Everyone was so busy and rushed off their feet. I had to just slot in and get on with it. I didn't have my own classroom and was moving around from day to day. This was another difficulty that I just had to overcome. Having no classroom and carrying books around all the time is a much bigger issue than most realise. It is much harder to be organised, and more difficult to start lessons in a way that settles classes. At Larne High you needed to start lessons well, but I had been dealt a difficult timetable with difficult classes and rooming. Fortunately, I had nothing to prove. I had achieved everything I ever set out to do in teaching with my time at ACS. My priority now was to be at home with my family, not to pursue my career and take it too seriously. I needed to work to pay the bills, and I would remain professional, but I would not judge myself by my performance when I was triple outside my comfort zone with a very difficult timetable.

I coped and managed to plug a gap for Larne High. I held the line and took the classes that otherwise would not have had a teacher. The school had advertised 3 times and no one suitable had applied. I was their last hope of finding someone who was willing to help. I would not be judging myself in the same way as I had judged my performance at ACS.

The kids always seemed to need to go to the toilet and want out of class. They weren't great at completing homework, and they could often get easily distracted. Despite all of this, most of them were decent and friendly enough. Some though were just defiant and unpleasant. For many, they just didn't like the curriculum and would have been better off in a system that taught them vocational skills instead of academic subjects. Many didn't plan on going to university, they needed skills that they could use more in their everyday lives. Larne High had introduced more practical subjects, but the curriculum imposed by the government was still too academic for too many of the pupils. Larne High did it's best with the difficult cards it had been dealt. A lack of funding, a UK curriculum that was too academic, and disengaged pupils who didn't care and who refused to behave.

I realised that my job satisfaction ultimately came from teaching my own subject of economics to students who wanted to learn. Larne High had become a job and was no longer my vocation. I was starting to see a life beyond the classroom. I would do this if necessary for a couple more years, but beyond that I wouldn't keep working in a school with such unruly pupils. It just wouldn't be worth it. Life is too short. I would either quit teaching or find a job outside of Northern Ireland where I could teach economics to students who were engaged and who wanted to learn. I still didn't know just where my career would end up taking me.

State education, like so many public services due to years of austerity, was getting to breaking point. The cost-of-living crisis, coupled with a decade of under investment in schools and cuts in the real pay of teachers, was pushing everyone to breaking point. Suddenly it became too much. The nurses went on strike, and then the teachers went on strike. It was a last resort to save public services and to get a fairer pay settlement. The government had refused to listen for 12 years, and it was time to either quit the profession or make a desperate last stand. Unfortunately, the Tories just wanted to cut costs, cut staff, and privatise everything, rather than invest in public services. It seems that workers in the public services would have to wait for a Labour victory in a General Election to see more investment in the hospitals and schools of the country, and to receive a fair pay award to make up for a fall of over 20% in pay in real terms since 2010. No wonder it was getting difficult to train and retain teachers. Not enough people wanted to work such long hours, looking after badly behaved children, for not enough pay. The strikes needed to be successful for the sake of the future of education in the country. It couldn't carry on like this. State schools were better funded back when I started my career in the mid 1990's and had gone downhill since I had been in the private sector from 2011 to 2022.

I was once more thinking that I would only teach as a permanent member of staff again in a country that appreciated and valued teachers. I could sub for a couple of years but beyond that I wasn't sure if I wanted to stay teaching in the UK any longer. I had been on the front line during Covid as a key worker, yet clearly nurses and teachers and many others were not properly valued and respected. It was time to strike. Not that I expected the Tories to listen. They were ideologically against the normal working people and just wanted to cut our public services, whilst simultaneously cutting taxes for the rich.

Tough times lay ahead. I needed to soldier on so to speak. I needed to go home in the evenings and just enjoy being with my family.

Another job came up in a grammar school teaching economics. I applied but it was obvious they wanted a younger, cheaper teacher. It was the Sledgehammer Day as I call it. The final acknowledgement that Northern Ireland would never give me a proper job again. Then came further budget cuts to education, and the next in line for cost cutting was the budget for substitute teachers. A sense of here we go again was taking hold. 15 years of budget cuts. The UK as a country did not value education. Or to be more precise, the Conservatives did not value state education and investing in the normal people. They were more interested in maintaining charitable status and tax loopholes for the private schools that their own kids attended.

I am feeling more and more like quitting the profession once my sons have both finished school or looking abroad to teach in a country that still values and respects teachers. Two more years to see which way my future path might lie. Two more years of most likely subbing on and off to see my boys through school. I call it semi-retirement. Schools in Northern Ireland it seems underutilise me as economics was axed in many schools back in 2008 due to The Entitlement Framework and cost cutting. I'm appreciated as a teacher only outside of Northern Ireland, but my family wouldn't follow me abroad, so I remain in the catch 22 situation of the last 15 years. I'm either semi-retired or estranged from my family.

The King's Coronation was a brief historical interlude, one which I was glued to on TV. Most of the people in the country are too young to have seen the previous Coronation back in 1953, so this was history in the making. I have grown to admire Charles for his dedication to protecting the environment. The historical day though quickly came and went, and then it was back to wrapping up the year at Larne High School. School exams loomed, and after that it would just be a couple more weeks of rowdy behaviour and then LHS would be over and finished with. I can't say that I would be too disappointed to leave. After ACS, I realised I no longer wanted a job which was more about crowd control of badly behaved children, I had done my time. I wanted to teach children who wanted to learn, not rude, disrespectful, and lazy children which unfortunately I had encountered too many of whilst at LHS. I am getting too old to tolerate this kind of abuse from children. I am a teacher to help kids learn, not to fight with them to get them to learn. Teaching in the UK has gotten worse on so many levels it seems since I started my career back in the 1990s.

Where next I wondered? What would September bring? I would just go away and enjoy my summer holidays and come back and see what would happen. There was nothing else for it. I still have a mortgage to pay and my own two sons at school to support. Two more years of subbing around Northern Ireland, and then if nothing acceptable comes up either quit teaching or teach abroad elsewhere.

Just before leaving Larne High, I decided to go back to London for a weekend and visit many of my old ACS friends, which for me was a nice touch. I only mention this due to the irony involved. I calculated that during my 10 years of travelling to London and back I'd taken about 750 flights. I therefore found it ironic that the only time I ever got stranded at an airport and had to sleep on the terminal floor for the night like a homeless person, was after I had finished my 10 years of commuting and on one of the first flights I had taken since. Sleeping on a terminal floor is most unpleasant and brings with it a feeling of vulnerability. What made this even more ironic was that it was a flight between London and Belfast. I had taken 750 flights and I'd never got stranded, although there had been some problems here and there, and then I take 1 flight afterwards and I get stranded. Really. Was someone trying to tell me something? Stay at home and don't go back to commuting. I am getting too old at 54 for the kind of stress and hassle that super commuting can bring.

Very soon afterwards my last day at Larne came, and I wasn't displeased to leave. It had been a tough year, and I had shown resilience. I had stuck it out, taught science and maths, and plugged the gap the school had needed. After a holiday in France, it would soon however be back to finding a new school. It was starting to feel like Groundhog Day, and I was getting weary. I needed a new school much like ACS, but I was never going to find that in Northern Ireland. Maybe it was time to just forget about my career and just enjoy my family instead. If only I could afford to retire.

Larne Grammar School Mixed Grammar Revisited

After the Summer my wife's school asked me in for a few days. The vice principal Paul was an old colleague back from my time at Bloomfield. I knew it would only be for a few days here and there, but it was nice to go in and see my wife at work and to get to know her school and work colleagues a little better. Larne Grammar is a lovely country grammar school. It is the kind of school in Northern Ireland I could happily work in, the kids are pleasant, and this makes all the difference. However, I couldn't stay long as Larne Grammar didn't have a full-time opportunity and I needed to pay the mortgage, it was however a nice brief interlude that helped me get through September.

I did ask both Paul the VP, and the headmaster why economics had been axed out of so many grammar schools in Northern Ireland. They both confirmed it was down to budget cuts since The Entitlement Framework, plus also that business studies had cannibalised economics over the years. Pupils see economics as a more difficult option than business studies. The two subjects are very different, but they are often perceived incorrectly as being similar due to the topics of money and finance. For me economics is an important subject that should be taught in all grammar schools, but I understood the budgetary restrictions that had been imposed on the headmasters over the years. Unfortunately, in addition CCEA the local exam board had also changed the A-level business studies specification to something very different to all the English exam boards specifications. They had changed it in such a way to make teaching CCEA A-level business studies very confusing and difficult to teach. With economics cut from many schools, and business studies changed in ways I couldn't effectively teach as I had done before, plus with a glut of cheap young teachers coming out of Stranmillis coupled with my advancing age and being more expensive to employ, then getting a full-time job in Northern Ireland was beyond my ability to obtain. I was an IB economics and IB business management teacher, an A-level teacher of business studies for the English boards, and an A-level economics teacher. Staying in Northern Ireland with my family meant accepting being a sub and being forcefully semi-retired. Such a waste, with all my IB experience from ACS Cobham, but my family came first before my career.

St Louise's Catholic Mixed Comprehensive

The phone rang again, this time a Catholic school called St Louise's on the Falls Road wanted me to come in and help. I had never imagined I would one day as an Englishman work on the Falls Road in West Belfast, right next to the milltown cemetery where two plains clothed British soldiers during the

Troubles had been dragged into and shot in the back of the head by the IRA. The peace process had come a long way in 25 years.

Everyone was friendly, except for a handful of the pupils who were poorly behaved.

I started by helping in business studies but after a few weeks was asked to help teach maths until Christmas. It was easy enough as I've taught KS3 maths and GCSE maths before. Walking around the corridor I'd hear pupils saying, 'That's the English teacher.' It seemed like I was a novelty again, reminding me of Northern Ireland back in 2000 when I had first arrived. The Falls Road felt like it was in some kind of time warp. The kids were interested in where I came from and were just being curious and friendly.

Apart from the few badly behaved kids, everything was ok. I'd get a coffee on the Lisburn Road, then walk 30 minutes to the school in the morning, and walk back in the afternoon getting my daily steps in. I was starting to feel better again, having lost weight from when I had left London and ACS. I was back to playing tennis, walking dogs, and having more energy. Finances were difficult as getting a permanent teaching job in Belfast was nigh on impossible at 54, but it was nice being at home with my family.

After the Halloween half-term there was a staff training day. I sat down in the school assembly hall waiting for it to start. The principal came in, welcomed everyone back and then the entire staff started doing Hail Mary's and crossing themselves. I'd never seen that before in all my 28 years to date of teaching. I guess there are still new experiences to be had, even after all these years in the classroom. To me all types of Christians are basically the same, so I just waited until they were done and then we all carried on with the training day. St Louise's clearly was not about to go multi faith and lose its Catholic identity as a school.

St Louise's originally had been an all-girls Catholic school run by nuns but had recently opened itself to accepting boys as well as girls. The school was rapidly changing, as a mixed comprehensive school is very different from an all-girls school run by nuns.

Every day at break and lunch I'd sit at the same table in the staffroom. It seemed everyone picked a table and stuck with the same one each day. I naturally gravitated to the table with mainly guys around my own age. It was quickly apparent that they disliked the Tories. I told them of how I had been on the Poll Tax march in about 1989/1990 and how I was against austerity economics. They soon accepted me with a welcoming grace. They had a dislike of the English Tories, but I clearly was no Tory, even though I was English. It was these staffroom chats whilst drinking peppermint tea that made the days at St Louise's pass more easily. When I think of St Louise's, it's these staffroom chats that shall always come first to mind.

Whilst at St Louise's the bank informed me that the 5-year fixed interest only mortgage was about to come to an end. The new mortgage deals on offer were hugely more expensive thanks to the Liz Truss disastrous mini budget. Monthly repayments would soon rise by over £400. With all our debts we needed more income. Years of pay cuts for teachers had taken its toll, and our finances were about to spiral dangerously even further downwards. Lorraine started planning on becoming a Counsellor in addition to teaching, and I took on some tutoring. After all these years of teaching we were both having to double job. No wonder teachers were still striking over pay and conditions. We were facing a retirement with no savings and no home. It seemed that as teachers we had helped many on to greater things, yet at the same time we'd been under appreciated and under paid by the government. It was finally approaching a breaking point unless we could somehow earn extra income.

The contract at St Louise's was only until the new year. I'd also need more regular employment very quickly once the short-term role at St Louise's was over. 2024 was starting to look financially precarious. My wife didn't want me to work away from home where I could earn a better income, and neither did I deep down in all honesty. I needed to be at home to help my youngest son especially finish school. I was however getting very worried about paying the mortgage.

The school Christmas exams came and went, and then it was nice to have a few days in a school with some festive cheer. At ACS in December students just finished their exams and then all departed immediately to all the far-flung corners of the earth for the holidays. At St. Louise's everyone lived in the nearby neighbourhoods, and there were a few days after the exams for some festive fun. It was time to watch a few Christmas movies and eat mince pies in the staffroom.

My short-term subbing of teaching maths then came to an end as I left for the Christmas holidays. I was back to daily subbing once more from January. I had no idea how we'd afford to pay the increased mortgage from January onwards. For now, I was just going to enjoy Christmas with my family.

The New Year came around and St Louise's asked me to do a few days more subbing, and luckily, I also started subbing at Belfast High School, a mixed grammar school much more to my liking.

Belfast High School Mixed Grammar

I soon started subbing more frequently at Belfast High. The kids were most pleasant and very quickly I bumped into Tona, one of my old Wallace friends from over 15 years earlier. She was now the head of chemistry at Belfast High. It was nice to see an old friend, and strangely helped me see my career in perspective. I could have just taught in one or 2 schools all my life and have been comfortable, or as had happened, I had taught in many schools and met many pupils and staff and had many more experiences. My unplanned and often unexpected career had enriched me far beyond what I would have become if I'd been allowed to play it safe and stay in the same comfortable school all my life. I was happy to have had my career where my soul had not been dulled into mundane routine year after year. Change and new experiences had kept my soul alive.

I was however most happy to be subbing at Belfast High school at this point in my career.

The head of business studies was off sick, and a young teacher fresh out of teaching college was holding the fort. He was soon joined by a student teacher who was on placement at Belfast High school. The pair of them coped admirably. They both had enthusiasm and energy, and more importantly the time to take work home and to stay up late each night preparing for the next day at school. Neither of them had children or parental responsibilities. I had come home from London to spend more time with my family and to help support them. I couldn't take work home and stay up late preparing lessons. Maybe semi-retirement was a better option. Maybe it was time to let the next generation have their turn. I'd done my time and already had a varied and interesting career. Offers continued to come in for working abroad, but maybe that was just a nice thought to finish my career. Maybe instead, it was better to just let my career fizzle out into permanent semi-retirement, to sub around the schools in Belfast with nice well-behaved kids.

Maybe it was better this way than to have taken a demanding role at a top foreign private international school. My career had effectively ended when I had been recalled by my family from ACS back to Belfast. Maybe it was time to hang up my boots and reflect on all I had achieved. Time to help my family and embrace my hobbies and interests. Life is too short and rushes by. Robbie was already in his first year at Queen's University in Belfast, and Jamie was in sixth form doing his A-levels. It only seemed like yesterday when they were both still small, whilst I was at Wallace all those years ago. Now they were both all but fully grown up. Where had all the years gone? They seemed to have flown by in a flash. At least I had done so much with my two boys growing up despite having been away for years during the week in London. We all had so many happy shared memories to cherish and had created loving bonds that would last a lifetime. It was nice to just be back home with my family.

Semi-Retiring

Luckily, I was turning 55 in a couple of months' time and a friend of Lorraine's told us we could cash in our pensions. This was the answer to our rapidly escalating dire financial situation. I filled out the forms for early retirement to cash in my private pension. We desperately needed the money. I turned on the coffee machine, put on an album from the 1980's, put my feet up and smiled. Everything was fine. It was my time. I needed to just let go of my career for the sake of my family.

The future now beckoned with all it's glorious uncertainty to a life beyond the classroom.

I spent an additional week at Edmund Rice College, a Catholic mixed state school where the staff and kids were pleasant, and then up until my 55th birthday and just beyond at Victoria College Belfast, my 10th grammar school in Northern Ireland. It was here at Victoria where I briefly used AI to help plan a few lessons for health and social care. It was so helpful and easy to use. Was this a glimpse of the future of teaching I wondered? Seeing as I was just waiting for my early retirement pension pay out to come through, I wouldn't have to worry about being replaced by artificial intelligence. That would be a concern for the next generation of teachers.

Victoria was the all-girls grammar school in my street, where my wife had attended as a girl. After all those years of commuting, I had truly come home.

It was the perfect school to officially semi-retire at. Everyone was lovely. I was finally back home in Marlborough Park, in my very own neighbourhood of the last 21 years. I could even walk home for lunch break if I so desired. Life in Northern Ireland couldn't get much better. I wondered how long it would last.

I had done 29 years, teaching 19 subjects across 26 schools. I had survived Covid, completed over 10 years of super commuting, and seen all there was to see in the classroom in the UK. It was a journey I could never have anticipated on that first day when I turned up to Hull University for my PGCE. I had so much to be proud of and nothing left to achieve, except perhaps to work abroad in a place like Dubai, Western Turkey, or the Cayman Islands.

As I took the short 5-minute walk back home from Victoria, I could hear the dogs barking as I approached the front door. It was time for their walk. Semi-retirement was clearly going to be busy. Busy is fine, I just hate being bored. I was finally ready for the next chapter.

But the spirit of Phoenix was still there. Would I arise yet one more time again in the future and write a whole new chapter in my teaching career? Probably not, but then in life you never know. I still had never worked abroad, yet I still primarily wanted to stay at home with my family. You can't do everything in life, you must choose. In my heart I know I shall always choose to be with my family, but sometimes the bank manager doesn't agree.

My old job teaching IB economics at ACS suddenly became available, and my many friends in London started asking me to go back. It was tempting as I missed all my old friends, but I had come home to get both my sons through school and their A-levels, and Jamie still had one more year of school left to complete. I had to see Jamie through school, that was my current purpose. Until then I couldn't pursue any career opportunities outside of Northern Ireland. By now it was obvious that I would never get a full-time economics teaching job again in Belfast, yet I was still too young to fully retire and still needed an income.

One more year of semi-retirement and subbing in Belfast, then I'd see what would come next. Once the pension payouts ran out, I could be forced to look for full time employment again outside of Northern Ireland. I wouldn't do anything without first discussing it with my wife Lorraine. I had a nagging feeling that one way or another the summer of 2025 would demand some tough choices and sacrifices. Best to enjoy the summer of 2024 first.

Martyn Agass, June 2024, Marlborough Park, Belfast.

For Robbie, Jamie, and Lorraine.

XXXX

Phoenix Time...... Rising from the ashes. What came next? Subbing at LGS in D&T & Science to take me to 2025, making it 30 years and 20 subjects, then.....I stayed with my family in NI and became the LGS Supersub. Carpe Diem. xx

After 30 years of teaching 20 different subjects across 26 different schools in both England and Northern Ireland, with over 10 years of commuting on planes as a teacher, these memoirs offer an insight into the teaching profession that very few others could match. State schools, private schools, international schools, brethren school, international college, adult night classes, all boy's schools, all girl's schools, mixed schools, protestant schools, catholic schools, and integrated schools. I've taught in them all and been an examiner. Discussions on education from a classroom teacher's perspective, and many stand out encounters over the years permeate throughout the work.

For anyone with any interest in the teaching profession and in schools, this sheds a light on what it is to be a classroom teacher, and how it is changing and has changed over the last 30 years. It shows schools of both the wealthy and the not so wealthy, schools from across the divide in Northern Ireland, international and British schools, and the closed community of the brethren.

It shows how teachers ultimately are not truly valued in the UK by Conservative governments and why so many end up leaving the profession. Many teachers though remain, as it is our vocation.

It's written in a light-hearted matter of fact style and tries not to lose its focus and pace throughout.